While a resident of Cuba from 1958-59 I became friends with Hemingway and it is from this friendship that I retrieved notes, photos, documents, and memorabilia from our residency in Progreso, Yucatan, Mexico that I have carefully crafted a quietly authoritative compendium and portfolio of materials to be utilized by THE HEMINGWAY HOUSE Bed and Breakfast of St. Augustine, FL. for such purposes as these facilities may deem appropriate and such shall be given freely and as gratis without any compensation. Indeed, the conveyance of these one-of-a-kind rare items to appreciative and responsible disciplines with the knowledge they will be appropriately displayed with dignified décor to the public thereby ensuring the preservation of the Hemingway Legend for all to appreciate is sufficien recompense for our family.

Respectfully,
Roger Shadow

Weekend at Hemingway's

With Photos and Illustrations
by Roger E. Shadow

WEEKEND AT HEMINGWAY'S

With Photos and Illustrations

by Roger E. Shadow

--

In collaboration with Gerald Houman Co-owner of the
HEMINGWAY HOUSE INN Bed & Breakfast
Saint Augustine, Florida

This book is dedicated to my loving wife Alicia. Her support and belief in me are manifested in this work becoming a reality.

Always, Roger

First Printing, 2015

ISBN 978-0-692-45498-5

Hemingway House Bed and Breakfast
54 Charlotte St
Saint Augustine, FL 32084
Hemingwayhouse,net

About the author

Roger E. Shadow, is a veteran of the Marion, Massachusetts to Bermuda races and has sailed the Caribbean extensively from the British Virgin Islands to the old whaling island of Bequia in the Grenadines. Also, over the years he was with the Florida State Board of Health; St. Regis Paper Co; and Nielsen Media Research. In those capacities he taught, including Hispanic Studies, wrote technical articles, curriculums and manuals. Currently, the author and his wife live on the West Coast of Florida and in Puerto Progreso, Yucatan, Mexico.

Acknowledgement

It is difficult to imagine any individual's work achieving completion without the input of others----and this text is no exception. Consequently, it is with humble thanks and deep appreciation that I herewith acknowledge Gerald (Jerry) Houman who collaborated with me on bringing this work to fruition. Jerry's patience and technical expertise are exemplary.

Muchas gracias, mi Amigo

WEEKEND AT HEMINGWAY'S

Table of Contents

Introduction

There is no prose stylist of the twentieth century who accommodates himself so adequately to an illustrated work as Ernest Hemingway. Indeed, my friend Papa, Pulitzer and Noble Prize winner as one of the most influential prose stylists owed his fame as much to his legendary life as to the power of his pen for he was more fascinating than any character he wrote about given he could at once be: hunter, lover, freedom fighter, drinker, brawler, fisherman and heroic activist.

And so it was as a resident of Cuba from 1958 to 1959 I met and became friends with Hemingway and it is from my initial long weekend visit and a return visit to Cuba that I have carefully crafted this informatively engrossing and quietly authoritative portrait of Papa. Further, the photographs of La Finca Vigia and memorabilia, which have never been seen before add a unique and evocative perspective of when Hemingway lived his last remaining years in Cuba. Thus, we have captured the terrace of La Finca where the author, drenched from a tropical downpour, initially met Hemingway the man among men and where Papa treated the author to a morning "body warmer"----a glass of straight Old Grand Dad bourbon and proceeded to hold forth on the art and science of fishing. Too, we have the dining room, den, and swimming pool of La Finca where the more sensitive, pensive and private Hemingway----the writer, the avid reader, the book collector, the incurable romantic expounded and held court on an array of topics that were boundless: immigration to the United States, Key West, coverage of wars, HUAC, Mayan History, love, celebrities, U.S. Department of State, Critics, etc. Moreover, we have photographs of Hemingway's beloved Pilar where for over 20 years he spent many blissful hours plowing el corriente del Golfo seeking the mysteries and his quest in its "hilero" ruling as lord and master as he roamed it's seas from the north coast of Mexico's Yucatan Peninsula to Bimini in the Bahama's where Papa in all his glory lived life to the maximum----in order to write about it. Also, we have the photographs of headstones marking the graves of Hemingway's favorite cats and dogs.

Warped and woofed into the Hemingway fabric are the photographs we have of El Floridita, Papa's "home away from home" in Vieja Habana. It was at El Floridita where Papa celebrated his nights----and some days----with his many friends and guest; e.g. Gary Cooper, Bill Walton, Spencer Tracy, Winston Guest, Ava Gardner, Archibald MacLeish, etc. Furthermore, it was at El Floridita where Jesus, the loquacious and most affable "keeper of the bar" and a personal friend of Ernest and Mary Hemingway proved to be the critical conduit for my connecting with Hemingway and it was Jesus who faithfully shared with me the fascinating history of El Floridiita----including the exact receipt for the legendary E. Hemingway Special Daiquiri.

The purpose of this text is to recapture a little of Hemingway's personal warmth, a bit of the sun-drenched life he loved to lead. The man who emerges from the text is the one partially most familiar to readers as the head of La Finca Crowd----in other words his Spanish Republican friends, the staff of La Finca and the "pescadoros" of Cuba: A man who liked a peaceful existence and who enjoyed the simple things of life. A Hemingway who did not share his secrets and who had not many friends to share them with anyway for he was a sensitive, tragic, solitary individual who, in many ways, was the exact opposite of his legend.

Excluded from this text is bibliographical information that is all too familiar and jaded and serves only to trivialize the monotonous, complicate the obvious and dull the interest of the reader by offering trite tidbits penned by people who never met or knew Hemingway! In contrast within the following chapters the reader will meet and hear one of the most exciting, enigmatic and stylistic geniuses of the last century who possessed an insatiable appetite for life. Gone is the arrogance Hemingway flaunted in his twenties, the braggadocio in his thirties and the swaggering he demonstrated in his forties.

This portrait reflects a sensitive and sympathetic image of a complex personality and a distinguished artist. Still, ever present is Hemingway himself and the hitherto puzzling components of his existence. His drive to endanger his life again and again, his epic battles with critics and his unapologetic assailing of the U.S. Department of Justice and it's Immigration Naturalization Service for what he said was their inbred policies of prejudice and bigotry exacerbated by politicians who were handicapped by natural immaturity.

While the enigma of Papa's life may never be solved, this portrait brings you the man as he was in his late fifties and as I knew him. Moreover, though Hemingway was not always an attractive man, his faults were an essential part of his character. Within the following pages I have illuminated some of the more intriguing and little known aspects of Papa's life in his twilight years: his treasured recipe's for his favorite foods and drinks, his view's on spear fishing as a sport, his loathing of U.S. Department of State's foreign policies towards Latin America with their priorities forged in arrogance and avariciousness, biographers, fascism, love, death, etc. Further, I have attempted to reveal a man of baffling complexity behind the myths and mystique of the Hemingway persona----volcanic, mercurial, frequently tortured, consumed with anxiety, yet always fascinating.

Here then is a portrait of my friend Hemingway whose reputation has survived his death and his detractors, and who is recognized as the most important and influential American novelist of the twentieth century and whose power and legend extend into our new millennium.
-

Chapter 1
Politics & *El Floridita*

In the late 1990s, Alicia and I went to Cuba and our Mexicana flight # 315 from Merida, Capital of the State of Yucatan, and Mexico to Havana, Cuba took approximately one and one half-hours. As our plane began its graceful decent to Havana's Aeropuerto Jose Marti -- the George Washington of Cuba-- we could see the emerald and azure waters of the Caribbean embracing the sugar white beaches with the ever swaying green coconut palms of Cuba's west coast shores. I commented to my wife Alicia who was accompanying me that although our home town of Progreso, Yucatan, Mexico was equally blessed with emerald and azure waters embracing our equally sugar white beaches with our ever swaying green coconut palms, Progreso did not enjoy the lush vegetation and undulated terrain that is reflected in Cuba. Although the Yucatan Straight separates the eastern most point of Cuba by less than eighty miles, the geographical differential is acutely detectable.

Following an uneventful landing and prior to deplaning I again inspected my travel documents cognizant of the fact that Cuban Immigration could be very pedantic with paperwork particularly for an American who previously lived in Cuba and now had residency in Mexico. As my wife was a Mexican National I anticipated no delays for her. Likewise, although I had -- and still have -- an FM3 for residency issued by the Secretaria de Gobemacion, Estados Unidos Mexicanos and had been assured by Cuba-Mex in Merida that I would experience no issues with Cuban Immigration, especially since I had listed as the purpose of my journey to Cuba was pleasure and to visit my old friend Hemingway's home; the legendary La Finca Vigia, in San Francisco de Paula. With Hemingway today still as popular in Cuba as when he lived and worked there over forty years ago, verification of same was immediately forthcoming as evidenced in the facial expressions and mannerisms of the Cuban official in charge of issuing visas in Merida upon my displaying for him a photograph of Papa and I together in front of La Finca. After an inspection of the photo and a barrage of excited questions the official was 'muy agradable y amistoso.'

To grasp Papa's continued popularity and reverence by the people of Cuba and Latin America, one will need to comprehend that among Hemingway's extraordinary abilities was his capacity to become 'one with the people.' For example, Hemingway was as much at ease sharing a bottle of 'backyard rum' with a skiff fisherman at a worn wooden table in a cantina as he was sipping vintage Fundador from a hand cut brandy snifter with a head of state in a revered private club. This Hemingway accomplished because he became one with people by simply eliminating the barrier that traditionally separates individuals and nations -- prejudice. This he did in Spain, France, Key West, Austria, Italy, and any place or country where he spent time or took residency. In contrast, because historically and currently both Cuban and U.S. foreign policies subordinate their domestic policies containing programs with social redeeming qualities to the ambitions of special groups these actions have created 'foreign policies by exception.' Not without precedent, Cuban foreign policies view the U.S. through the eyes of fear thereby providing a myopic perspective of their 'neighbor to the north.' Likewise, in lieu of the Cuban governments wearisome haranguing reproving the U.S. for all of Cuba's social and economic ills, then varnished truth discloses the reality that the leadership of the Cuban government is void of any understanding of its sister and brother nations throughout the real world who participate in a financial environment wherein the 'coin of the realm' is functional macro and micro economics raised from a heretofore art to a complex science wherein Marx and Engels stand as anachronisms. Notwithstanding, the U.S. in its courtship with Latin American nations has always been more interested in the wedding than the marriage.

Indeed, this naked truth is predicated on the fact that a distinctive quality of the 'American Persona' is that of the white Angelo Saxon Protestant. Accordingly, and tragically, in America's 'Garden of Liberty' where purportedly grows 'Democracy' so also grows well the strangling weeds of hate that has, and continues, to choke Hispanic people. Further, because U.S. politicians suffer from the illusion that they, and only they, have a monopoly on righteousness, any nation or its leader who expresses a position contrary to that espoused by our government is branded as a threat to America's National Security." And one should not ask about the Evil Angel of terror and death that in the past we have unleashed upon the Hispanic peoples of

Guatemala, Panama, Mexico, Nicaragua, El Salvador, and others, all in the name of Democracy,' 'Freedom,' and 'National Security.'

Both great nations, Cuba and the U.S. continue on a perilous passage plotted by leaders who are handicapped by immaturity in the art and skill of statesmanship. This, because the leaders of Cuba and the U.S. learn not from the lessons of the past, they fear the future, and do not understand the present. Subsequently, when and only when, the people of both Cuba and the U.S. demand from their leadership that humanistic values not be subordinated to political/economic ambitions will both great countries be on a charted course of hope navigating for the intersection of enlightenment and understanding with each other and their family of global nations.

With the folly of politics still racing through my mind I presented my Mexican FM3 and Cuban visa to an immigration officer whereupon he quickly inspected both documents, affixed the official Cuban stamp, and returned both documents to with a smile and the single comment, "Bienvenidos a Cuba!" Alicia's passage through Cuban immigration was routine. Next, Cuban customs, "aduanas Cubano," presented but a formality with the most significant item being the determination of how much actual cash currency we were physically carrying with us. With satisfactory verification of our combined total cash assets ascertained, we cleared customs and proceeded out of Aeropuerto Jose Marti to where one of the large Swedish tour buses were awaiting the arrival of new foreign visitors. Recently acquired by the Cuban Ministry of Tourism, the buses were complete with sanitary facilities, water fountains, music, air conditioning, tinted windows, carpeting, etc.

Relaxed comfortably in the spacious tour bus upholstered seats Alicia and I were taken towards our hotel in Central Havana, the Hotel Vedado. Traversing the main avenues and boulevards I noted the distinct renaming of many of the famous landmarks that had been witness to so much of the Caribbean's violent, exciting, romantic, tragic, but always colorful and interesting history.

Beginning in early 1959 Fidel's propaganda policy of bestowing accolades on behalf of his loyal troops, affectionately known a los vienteseis de julio hombres, is reflected in the renaming of these easily recognizable landmarks. For example, what was historically known as Plaza de la Republica is now Plaza de la Revolucion; formally Calle Simon Bolivar is now Calle Salvador Allende. Further, other areas and facilities are presently identified as: Parque Lenin, Camilo Cienfuegos, Diez de Octubre, etc. So much for the accuracy of historical sites as rewritten by dictators, I thought to myself.

As the searing sun shorn through the Royal Palm trees lining the avenues and boulevards and reflected off the many pastel colored buildings and what with the avenues and boulevards clogged with thousands of Cubans peddling bicycles that were imported from China as part of a Cuban sugar exchange, the scene created was somewhat surrealistic.

Following our arrival at the Hotel Vedado and with checking in completed, the representative from the Cuban Tourist Ministry who had accompanied us on the bus, escorted all the newly arrived guest to a private room where the official Bienvenido a Cuba speech was given followed by all present being provided with a glass of the official drink of Cuba -- rum.

Immediately following our politically correct welcome ceremonies Alicia went to our room that was somewhere between unpretentious and Spartan to freshen up. I went outside of our hotel to make arrangements for a Turistaxi to take us the following day to Hemingway's home, La Finca Vigia, in San Francisco de Paula. Since vehicle fuel is at a premium in all Cuba, the Turistaxis congregate almost exclusively at, near, and around the hotels of Havana as opposed to 'cruising' about seeking fares. Accordingly, as I exited the front door of the hotel I took note of a smiling, ingratiating looking young Turistaxi driver who carried an aura of confidence about him. Thus, wading through a gathering of Turistaxi drivers who were shouting, and assuring me, that each one in turn could secure for me, if I were so inclined, the very best prices for black market Cuban cigars, rum, and if I had a propensity, female companionship. With a smile and a "Gracias, pero no gracias," I continued making my way to the handsome young man I had initially spotted. Then, shaking hands we introduced ourselves whereupon the young driver declared himself as Carlos Armando. Following introductions I inquired of Carlos if he knew of and could take Alicia and I to my old friend Hemingway's home.

Officially designated as a National Museum of Cuba, Museo Hemingway, a.k.a. La Finca Vigia is located approximately 15 miles southeast of Viejo Habana and approximately seven miles south of the Gulf of Mexico. Cheerfully and confidently Carlos assured me he knew El Museo Hemingway and would be delighted to take Alicia and I there. Next, Carlos asked if we would be interested in visiting the modem "Marina Hemingway", a.k.a. Hemingway Marina located approximately 11 miles to the west of the intriguingly enchanting and world famous Hotel Nacional reposed on Havana's legendary and romantic "El Malecon." I responded with "Tal vez -- despues." Concluding our arrangements, Carlos and I agreed to meet in front of the Hotel Vedado the next day at 10:00 a.m.

The following morning was a bright sunny day with a brisk breeze blowing from the northeast off the Gulf of Mexico, over the Malecon and down the traffic arteries of North Havana. After a hearty breakfast of eggs, bacon, fruit juice, bread, and the always cafe Cubano con leche y azucar provided by the Hotel Vedado, Alicia and I proceeded to the hotel front door and exited. Contrary to most American's popularly held belief that the "Latino" concept of time is always manana, the ever felicitous Carlos was punctual and eagerly waiting for us.

From the Hotel Vedado Carlos proceeded north for three blocks, pass the Hotel Nacional, then turned right onto Avenido Antonio Macea, a.k.a. El Malecon. As we drove along El Malecon I recalled many of the sights; impressive today as they were back in the late 1950's when I first saw them: the monument Antonio Maceo, the Hotel Deauville in Viejo Habana and across the entrance to Bahia de la Habana in La Habana del Este, El Castillo de Los Tres Santos Reyes Magas del Morro, a.k.a. Morro Castle.

Notwithstanding, a reminder of Fidel's presence are the well maintained and color contrasting signs that today still punctuate the landscape of El Malecon with hackneyed and banal radical political slogans that proclaim: "This Land Is 100% Cuban!" "Cuba, Si. Yanqui, No!" "Socialism Or Death!" What Fidel fails to state is the fact that only "Yanqui" dollars are permitted by any visiting tourist as a legal tender in Cuba, that he eagerly awaits the US Treasury Dept. checks paid to Cuban Nationals who work at the US Guantanamo Bay facility, and enjoys the large influx of "Yanqui" dollars into Cuba funneled in by the tens of thousands of exiled Cubans living in the US who routinely send money to relatives who are still in Cuba. Like all dictators, Fidel amplifies the lies because the truth is so ugly! In reality such trite revolutionary graffiti only serves to deface a beautiful tropical panorama vista and produce among many Cubans who frequent North Havana, chuckles and snickers.

When our Turitaxi reached the northeast point of El Malecon, pass the Castillo de San Salvador de La Punta and was traveling southeast on Avenido Carlos M. Cespedes, a.k.a. Avenido del Puerto, passed the harbor of Bahia de La Habana one could witness large numbers of commercial freighters at anchor -- rusting from lack of maintenance and use. This, a tragic and ludicrous consequence of the U.S. embargo and economic sanctions against Cuba that have their roots in the rancid rhetoric of emotionally unstable politicians and venomous fanatical hate groups in Florida, who with their money purchase -- or at minimum lease these politicians. To this end, the U.S. trade embargo against Cuba -- that in reality is a trade embargo against ourselves -- represents yet another calamitous inconsistency in U.S. foreign policy that we have forced upon a Latin American nation. Although the embargo was enacted 40 years ago and has entangled over a half dozen U.S. presidents, the net results when scrutinized discloses a policy that has yielded only diplomatic, economic, and humanistic bankruptcy for us. Consequently, Fidel continues as Comendodar of Cuba while the embargo inflicts only suffering, agony, and pain upon the children, the old, and the infirm of Cuba. Moreover, internationally the embargo has placed us in the absurd situation of continuously reiterating contradictory statements of our position relevant to the embargo. Thus, when we belch platitudes about refusing to trade with, " ... a nation that abuses human rights, does not hold free elections restricts individual freedoms, and has not adequately secured the future for the Cuban people ..." the serious practitioners of statesmanship among our family of world nations increased our aid to North Vietnam, provided assistance to North Korea, escalated our technical support to the Arab Nations, and concluded a major trade agreement with Red China! Likewise, in addition to our commercial loss suffered as a direct result from the economic embargo, we have earned the malice and condemnation of esteemed world leaders. Accordingly, as our neighbor to the north, Canada, and our long time friends such as Sweden, Italy, France, Spain, England, Belgium, etc. enjoy a brisk economic trade with Cuba, while we in the U.S. like a spoiled rich brat who can not have their way, sit and pout. Indeed, how tragic that we here in the U.S. with over a quarter of a billion population that is diverse and homogeneous should be refused the opportunity of participating with another family nation in the socioeconomic and cultural activities and, that of a neighbor nation, with close historical ties to us with less than 90 miles separating our shores because a few politicians have chosen to insulate themselves with the darkness of ignorance so as not to be touched by the illumination of enlightenment. Such irresponsibility serves only to verify that as the statesman commits to solving the problems of today for the benefit of tomorrow's generations, the politician plots to get reelected. Hence, there is an old Mexican proverb that says, "Before we unlock the door to tomorrow's understanding we must first find the key to yesterday's wisdom." Sadly, some politicians are not even aware that the key is missing -- hardly poster material for statesmanship and illumination.

With the process of pondering preposterously practiced politics all but receded in the back of my mind, I settled a bit more comfortably in the back seat of our Turistaxi as effusive, but always cordial Carlos was conversing away about the large influx of European tourist visiting Cuba, especially from Denmark, England, Canada, Germany, Sweden, Italy, Spain, France, etc. Carlos acknowledged that aside from the much needed revenue he received to further his education he enjoyed the tourist as an information resource as he learned much about the customs, culture, and unique ways of life in different lands. As Carlos turned onto Czda de Guines, driving in a southeast direction, and Alicia taking in the sights and talking to Carlos, I recalled the single defining moment that was responsible for bringing together Hemingway and I -- El Floridital

"Ah, El Floridita -- one of the world's truly great watering holes!" so proclaimed one of its best and most famous customers and patrons -- Ernest Hemingway. Still, to fully understand the acclamations given to El Floridita -- Papa's "home away from home" we need to peek at its past which was partially provided by Hemingway to me and the balance by a loquacious, humorous, kindly, and very knowledgeable mixologist at El Floridita named Jesus Humberto.

"La Historia de La Habana Vieja" records that more than a century and a half ago, in the simple uncomplicated days of 1819, a typical chophouse rose above the walls at the entrance of the Monserrate Gate in what now is Viejo Habana (Old Havana). It was a pleasant grilled structure, a rendezvous for beaux, musicians, army officers, attorneys, actors, gentleman of culture and honor, desirous to partake of the delicious and tasty "mixed gin" of cherry Brandy. Ladies in their carriages under bright silken parasols sipped delicious brandies while being courted by their gallant knights.

This ideal venerated place was called the "La Pina de Plata" -- The Silver Pine. This was over a century and a half ago. Now, with the passing of years,

The Silver Pine facing Albear Square, overlooking the old colonial streets filled with traditions of its romantic past, has been renamed El Floridita. The Silver Pine and El Floridita cafe still stand, the former in our remembrance, the latter in the reality of life's daily toll, serving the public, businessman, scholars, professionals, members of government, and the most beautiful or elegant women, with exquisite whipped fruit juices and most delicate wines and cocktails.

The Silver Pine chophouse was transformed during the days of the American occupation into headquarters for the good Yankee tipplers. The bartenders gradually modernized the simple drinks of our ancestors and the valuable efforts added to the bright talent of conctante, have converted the glorious and historic comer into a refuge of art and poetry.

The frozen Daiquiri originated with one of El Floridita's previous owners, one Don Constantino Ribalaigua and although a world famous drink is served nowhere as in its old and romantic cradle; thus the motto of El Floridita, "La Cuna del Daiquiri" (the cradle of the Daiquiri). To this end, Don Constantino Ribaliqua held that as the modem cocktail is said to be the poetry of liquor, it's essence and fragrance is as that of a subtle flower. The delicate crystal of the cocktail glasses enables you to enjoy all the good that exist, leaving the hardship of daily life forgotten. The scenery is unsurpassed beauty. Pain is overlooked; Love sweeter and tender. THE COCKTAIL IS SPIRITUALISTIC!

At the beginning of the 'dry era' noted magazines in the United States and England wrote that unfortunately for the present and future generations the art of the cocktail would remain, as did ancient culture in Europe during the invasion of the barbarous, safely revered in its most sacred temples, viz: The American Bar in Paris, facing the Gran Opera (at the rear of the Cafe de la Paix) and the Bar Restaurant El Floridita in Havana, Cuba.

Today as over a century and a half ago, erected over the same old stones of The Silver Pine the "Cocktail Cathedral" where "constante" officiates, stands amid the traditional streets for the delight of good drinkers and continues to be the gathering place of men and women who can distinguish the good wines and drink with ecstasy the essence of a cocktail, the sweet symbol of a high and elaborate civilization. The Silver Pine, El Floridita -- 'La Cuna del Daiquiri" -- 1819 to the present -- over a century and a half of fine standing. Cocktails, wines, refreshments, ices, smiles, flirtations, happiness, negotiations, love, all of this over the same old stones, facing the same unchangeable scenery, under the same warm, blue sky -- and so it was on a warm humid tropical evening in early September of 1958 that as I was leaving my hotel, the Hotel Nueva Isla at which I was paying $2.50 U.S. a night, located on the western fringe of La Habana Vieja that I inquired of the registration manager, Luis, a sincere and honest soul, if he could recommend a restaurant bar that had air conditioning. Luis flashed a broad smile revealing some bad teeth -- and confidently proclaimed, "El Floridita, (which I had previously heard about), en el esquina de Obispo y Monserrate en La Habana Vieja. No es muy lejos desde aquil", Luis assured me. As the Hotel Nueva Isla was on the comer of Monte and Suarez, only a few blocks southeast of the "magic corner" that Luis had informed me about I left the hotel and on foot proceeded towards the Museo National de Historia Natural and eventually ended up at the front door of what promised to be a "wonderful place to cool off and wet the whistle."

Entering through El Floridita's unpretentious front door I spotted an empty stool at the far end of the bar and sauntered towards it, climbed on, and made myself comfortable enjoying the functioning and refreshing air conditioning. Although I was cognizant of the fact that "La Cuna del Daiquiri" was Hemingway's most favorite bar in all Cuba and was legendary throughout the world for their frozen Daiquiri's, I nevertheless informed the barman I would like a very cold bottle of Hatuey -- the official beer of Cuba. However, I was eventually persuaded by the young, husky, garrulous, but amicable keeper of the bar named Jesus Humberto after his evoking a dazzling blend of rhetoric and pooh-pooh dust to try El Floridita's 'E. Hemingway' Special Daiquiri which I was guaranteed was made from Papa's own recipe. Hence, giving Jesus an affirmative to proceed he engaged in a blend of barman's sorcery and incantations and presented me with the results. I consumed the daiquiri and assured Jesus that indeed, it was a great drink. I ordered a second 'E. Hemingway' Special and requested from Jesus that he make the delightful creation with a full explanation leaving nothing to chance in the Keeper of the Bar's World of Black Mixology. This, Jesus graciously and generously provided to me and in perfect English:

E. HEMINGWAY'S SPECIAL
DAIQUIRI:
    2 liberal ounces of Bacardi rum
    1 teaspoon grapefruit juice
    1 teaspoon maraschino
    The juice of 1lime/lemon
    Frappe ice
    Shake well and serve frappe

Jesus did share with me that the name 'E. Hemingway' Special Daiquiri was used with the tourist; however, among the Cubanos, the drink was referred to as "Daiquiri a La Papa."

As I savored my second 'Caribbean Concoction' I began to study the numerous photos of Papa that were displayed on the walls of El Floridita, The more I continued to examine the portraits the more they became a collage of scenes that were spectacular -- Venice and Cortina d' Ampezzo in Italy, Pamplona and Madrid in Spain, Paris and Cap d' Antibes in France, Voralberg and Schruns in Austria, The PILAR and Sloppy Joe's in Key West, the Serengeti Plain and Tanganyika in Africa -- and the gallery of characters associated with the locales represented a panorama of the literary and famous of the twentieth century-- Stein, Fitzgerald, Picasso, Rawlings, Pound, Sara and Gerald Murphy, etc. Indeed, I mused Hemingway was not simply an individual, but a way of life, an era. Further, I pondered here is a man deeply divided against himself, with the most conspicuous split separating the literary genius of worldwide fame, and man of feeling on the one hand, from the adventurer, sportsman, and man of action on the other.

Continuing to savor my second 'E. Hemingway" Special' I returned to my barstool and acknowledged to Jesus my admiration for his skills as a mixologist whereupon Jesus and I began exchange the usual nuggets of bar keep/customer information. Why had I come to

18

Havana? Maybe I came to acquire material for a non-fiction book? Where had I come from? I explained, "The West Coast of Florida." Jesus in turn related that he came from East Mexico and that he learned English from his father who was an American. As Jesus and I conversed my eyes would rivet to the spectacular photos of Papa on the walls. Then, with my curiosity becoming unbridled I inquired of the gregarious Jesus if Papa had recently been into El Floridita. Jesus acknowledged that Papa had only several nights before accompanied by some friends who had been with him shooting at the Cerro Hunting Club. I listened, ordered a third 'E. Hemingway Special,' and lamented to Jesus as to how I truly would liked to have met and spoke with Papa. "Maestro" Mixologist Jesus momentarily ceased slicing his large pile of dark green limes, looked and motioned with his large head in the direction of the dining area and suggested I use the wall phone and call La Finca Vigia, Startled, I focused on Jesus and with a blend of surprise and vexation -- more surprise than vexation -- stated that I did not have the phone number for La Finca; obviously Hemingway did not know me and that to call would in all probability be considered presumptuous and in bad form. Jesus calmly offered that the Havana operator would provide me with the phone number and that a call to would not necessarily be considered audacious as people frequently called La Finca form El Floridita. Massaging Jesus' pragmatic phrases I concluded that a call from me to La Finca, from my perspective admittedly bold, held the promise of everything to be gained and nothing to be lost.

Subsequently, I left my bar stool with my third 'E. Hemingway Special' half filled and secured atop a napkin and with pen and paper moved to the left where the wall phone was located near to the entrance of the restrooms. Removing the phone from the receiver and in a most professional manner I asked the Havana operator for the telephone number of La Finca. True to what Jesus had assured me I secured with ease the phone number and asked the operator to place the call for me. This she did. After the phone rang piercingly for perhaps a dozen times it was answered by a woman who spoke in English with a friendly but authoritative voice. In response to the woman's brisk "Hello!", I replied with "Good evening," and proceeded to introduce myself with a delivery that must have sounded and came across as dialogue representing a hybrid between gushing and babbling what with my rapid explanation that I was not a critic, reporter, or biographer; but a young humble would be writer in Havana who has always greatly admired Mr. Hemingway as a person, his works as a writer, and would be most grateful for the opportunity to meet the legendary "Papa". Nearly out of breath, it occurred to me that I did know with whom I was speaking. I confessed this ignorance to the voice on the phone with, "Please excuse my bad manners, but with whom am I speaking?" The reply came back, "Mary Hemingway."

"*Mrs. Mary!*" I said to myself and resolved that, "*Well Roger, you blew this one with your ramblings!*" However, Mrs. Mary -- Papa's fourth, last, and perhaps most controversial wife instructed me to wait a moment, and, after what seemed to be an eternity she returned to the phone with the statement, "Mr. Hemingway will see you tomorrow morning at 9:00 a.m. -- and bring an overnight bag."

Dumb founded by the invitation I proceeded to dig my hole of awkwardness deeper by apologizing for the call thereby snapping defeat out of the jaws of victory by relating how I was speaking with a friendly bar keep at El Floridita who had given me courage to call when Mrs. Mary interrupted me with loud laughter and commented, "Oh, you must have been speaking with Jesus! He's so adorable and precious, but, oh my, how he does love to chat away!" She terminated the call with, "Remember, 9:00 a.m. tomorrow morning -- sharp!"

I stood looking at the wall phone in a state of euphoria and experiencing a "willing suspension of disbelief" when the telephone which I had been holding to my ear begin to buzz loudly. Composing myself I hung the telephone up and walked back to where my half-full -- or half-empty -- glass of 'E. Hemingway Special' was awaiting me. The loquacious Jesus was still slicing his large pile of dark green limes; however, when he observed my contentment he flashed a confident smile. He made no inquiry regarding the success -- or failure -- of my telephone call and uttered not a word until I had drained my daiquiri whereupon he asked, "Uno mas?"

"No, thank you," I responded as I paid my bill and ensured there was a generous propina included and proceeded to remove myself from the barstool. Then, as I began to walk towards the exit door Jesus asked, "What are doing for the weekend?"Turning around I looked at my jolly bar keep, grinned, and quipped; "I'm going to visit Papa!" Jesus displayed a smile that was somewhere between angelic and impish, opened his arms wide and said, "Como no?"

Returning to the Nueva Isla I engaged the always agreeable Luis for the specifics as to the most efficient -- and economic -- means of transportation from La Habana Vieja to La Finca Vigia in San Francisco de Paula. The helpful Luis, who was my navigator around much of Havana, related that a bus to San Francisco de Paula stopped mid way between the Cuban Presidential Palace and the Cuban Museum of Natural History approximately every half hour beginning at 5:00 AM until 2:00 AM. As this location was about a ten minute casual walk from the Hotel Nueva Isla, the geographical locations presented no problem. Further, Luis stated that La Finca Vigia was approximately a 15 minute walk northeast from where the bus would leave me off.

With these nuggets of information tucked away in my memory I bid the informative Luis, "Buenas noches y nos vemos manana por la manana." I took the hotel elevator to the sixth floor, exited, and walked to my room located in the northwest corner of the hotel building. Then, entering my adequate lodging, I proceeded to remove my clothing, carefully folded and placed them on the chair, set my old alarm clock for 5:30 a.m. entered my bed, adjusted the pillow with my forearm and slipped into a deep untroubled sleep -- thanks, in part to the 'E. Hemingway Specials.'

The old alarm clock that I had set went off punctually with a shrill that sliced through the tranquility of the newborn tropical morning. Completing a brisk shower in the all white and blue tile bathroom I quickly dressed, took my overnight bag that I had fastidiously packed the previous night, left my room, and began walking towards the elevator. However, on this unique morning I walked pass the elevator to the communal balcony of the hotel that faces north and is located at the end of the hotel's hallway overlooking the picturesque and world famous 'Prado' of Havana that effectually divides Havana to the west from Old Havana to the east.

Walking to the railing of the balcony that was void of any guest at this early hour I witnessed to the northeast the initial rays of the day's new born sun that was emerging out of the warm pastel waters of the Florida Straits, and rapidly becoming more intense I ascertained that this morning was revealing itself to be a balmy tropical day in Havana with the northeast winds (El Nortes) of the previous evening and very early this morning having driven off most of the lingering humidity.

As no food was served at the Hotel Nueva Isla, the good Luis had heretofore suggested that if desired "un bueno typical desayuno Cubano -- y cual es muy barato, I should go to El Resterante La Selva which was directly across from the hotel. A typical Cuban breakfast consists of: Cuban coffee with large quantities of milk and sugar, Cuban bread, butter, and marmalade, (cafe cubano con leche y azuca, pan cubano con mantequilla, y marmalada). Likewise, Luis had informed me that the bus for San Francisco de Paula stopped punctually every hour on the half hour in front of the Presidential Palace which faced east on the Prado approximately five blocks north of the Hotel Nueva Isla.

Sitting anxiously at the counter El Restaurante La Selva I finished the last sip of my cafe Cubano, paid the modest breakfast check of fifty cents, picked up my overnight bag, and began walking north on the Prado at a brisk pace to where the bus stop was located. Then, to my left I spotted the congenial Luis who bid me un buen viaje at which point I hailed to him, took out my camera, and recruited Luis to take a photo of me on the Prado "por suerte." This he did -- and graciously. With the passing of approximately 10 minutes, and giving validation to what the informative Luis had told me, a tired and weary bus bound for San Francisco de Paula punctually rolled up to the designated bus stop sign with breaks squeaking, squealing, and smoking. Boarding the bus I paid my "10 centavos" and took a seat in the rear, placed my overnight bag on the floor of the bus between my feet and relaxed. Continuing onward the made it's appointed stops at the pre-designated locals until it reached Cespedes (del Puerto) Avenue at which point the portly driver began winding up the RPMs of the bus' exhausted old diesel engine in each gear creating large clouds of gray-black fumes that choked the women who were out early to do their daily shopping at a local mercado.

Chugging, wheezing, and coughing along Via Blanca Ruta towards the fishing village of Cojimar in a serpentine manner the bus manager to continue to make progress in a southeast direction, and, being comfortable in my seat I enjoyed the site, landmarks, and scenery along the route.

With the passing of approximately 40 minutes after I had boarded my bus it entered the Village of San Francisco de Paula. Then, coming to a screeching halt in front of a small mercado I stepped off the emphysematous vehicle onto a partially paved and very dusty road. Spotting an old vendor of fruits I asked if he knew of -- and could direct me to -- Hemingway's La Finca Vigia. Obligingly, the old vendor pointed and provided me with details whereupon I began heading in the direction to which he had indicated.

As I proceeded to walk along the roadside I enjoyed observing the activities of the village. An old woman peeling oranges in the doorway of her home, a small boy chasing after lizards, a young woman beating her laundry, an old man repairing fishing lines, shaggy curs running about, and so and so forth went the daily life of the village. After approximately 15 minutes of walking at a 'Cuban Pace' -- which is somewhere between a 'Caribbean Cadence' and a 'Tropical Saunter' I spotted a classical Spanish farmhouse atop a high hill that had a winding road that led from the front terrace down to the road which I was on and who's entrance to the road was secured by two large white wooden gates. From the description given to me by the old fruit vendor I knew it was La Finca Vigia.

Just as I reached the white wooden gates a typical downpour began. Then, following Mrs. Mary's instructions I pushed one of the gates open and started walking up the winding road that was -- and still is -- flanked on both sides by tall beautiful Royal Palm trees. Although the rain increased in intensity, I noticed to my left blue skies signaling that this inconvenient tropical rain would be of short duration. Clutching my overnight bag tightly and somewhat oblivious to the rain, that now, as suddenly as it had begun began to diminish; I continued my walk up the inclined road that would take me to La Finca's front door. As I plodded onward and upward I began reflecting more intensely upon how I would initially react to this Pulitzer and Nobel Prize winner who was the most admired and controversial writer of the twentieth century what with his worldwide fame as a literary genius, his stormy relations with family, critics, rivals, and his epic battles with his closest friends; every option of verbal engagement danced through my mind -- condescending, defensive, acquiescent, etc. With the heretofore tropical downpour now reduced to a sprinkle, I raised my head up from its former downward position where I had kept it to keep the rain out of my face as I followed the lines of Royal Palms upward. Suddenly, approximately 30 feet in front of me were the wide steps of the terrace that led up to the portal and front door of La Finca. Then, performing like a Russian Ballot Dancer I began prancing my way upward and over the flat stones of the steps surface due to the large and numerous piles of vintage and new animal droppings. Tip toeing my way to the front door and without any forethought I automatically knocked firmly about a half dozen times. As I stood wiping the rain off my forehead, eyebrows, and nose the door swung swiftly open and before me stood Hemingway. As I crossed the threshold of the door I would leave Hemingway the legend and meet Hemingway the fact.

Illustrations:

In 1959, $2.50 (per night) could secure a hotel room overlooking the Prado, Havana's major street for shopping, restaurant, and nightlife.

"EL FLORIDAITA is one of the world's truly great watering holes!!!!" ~ Papa

EL FLORIDAITA , "The Cradle Of The Daiquiri", located in Old Havana, was one of Hemingway's "home away from home". It was here that Papa played host to luminaries such as: Gary Cooper, Maxwell Perkins, Ava Gardner, Archibald MacLeish, Ingrid Bergman, and others.

26

The Author pictured during the early morning prior to his departure to Hemingway's La Finca Vigia. The always agreeable and upbeat Luis, Manager of the Hotel Nueva Isla, in Old Havana, took the photo.

Diez centavos, the equivalent of .10 cents, was the fare on a local bus from Havana to Hemingway's La Finca Vigia, San Francisco de Paula; approximately a one hour – and an unforgettable ride in 1958

September, 1958, La Finca Vigia San Francisco de Paula, Cuba; The author with his friend Hemingway. The Author found 'Papa' more interesting than any of the characters Hemingway wrote about.

The village of San Francisco de Paula provided for Hemingway the tranquility to rest what he called, "My delicate instrument – my brain". In the village Papa managed a local baseball team and the villagers then, as now, related that regardless of how busy their world famous resident would be, he always found to visit and talk with them.

Chapter 2
Hemingway, Old Grand Dad, La Finca Vigia, Lunch, San Francisco de Paula and More Good Stuff

Hemingway, at 58 years of age, physically reflected a vintage adventurer rough hewed out of raw burliness, one who had spent a lifetime going where he wanted to go and doing what he wanted to do. To this end, the numerous lumps, bumps, and scares that adored his sun tanned body personified canceled checks that characteristically confirmed payment in full for the way he lived. Moreover, Papa's six foot plus frame carried the 200 plus pounds proportionately void of the proverbial "pot belly," "midriff bulge," and "love handles," so indigenous to many men who are in the autumn of their years. Likewise, Hemingway's thin hair was gray as was the tangled, craggy, mass of foliage that covered his face; yet which did not hide his warm eyes that were like two large blotters that absorbed everything they observed. Further, his wide mouth was molded in an impish fashion at the ready to announce some mischievous undertaking. Too, for a first time greeting Papa's attire was something less than agreeable. His hair was in disarray, his once white guayabera (the short loose shirt-jacket indigenous to, and worn by, Latin American men) was gray and frayed, his tan shorts were ill fitted, droopy, and soiled with what appeared to be grease, and his brown leather loafers were scruffy and cracked. He wore no socks. Papa's warm blotter eyes beheld me standing before him -- with the early morning tropical deluge dripping off me.

From within this burly body I expected to hear a deep bellowing voice emerge from his barrel chest; however, my expectation was quickly modified for when Hemingway spoke he did so in an elevated voice.

"Christ! You're soaking wet!" Papa pronounced.

"Typical tropical downpour," I stammered still clutching securely my overnight bag.

"Shit, just don't stand there! Come on in!" Papa beckoned with his hand and head.

This was my introduction to Hemingway -- not even a handshake!

Stepping through the front doorway and into the hall, I placed my overnight bag on the tile floor. Standing next to me Hemingway began speaking in the rapid Spanish indigenous to Cuba and soon a middle aged black man of average height and built appeared in a crisp light blue shirt, light tan pants, and brown shoes. His hair was curly, cut short, and he had sparkling clear cheerful eyes and ivory teeth that flashed when he smiled. He sported an old Hamilton wristwatch with an old, sweat stained leather band. Hemingway introduced me to him as Juan Pastor, Papa's "unofficial, official man of the house."

Again, in the rapid Spanish, Hemingway instructed Juan to bring me a dry towel and shirt. To this gesture I mildly protested given the fact that I would dry off shortly. Hemingway silently dismissed my protestation and motioned to Juan to "carry on." Consequently, Juan returned with a large faded pink towel and one of Papa's white guayaberas whereupon I was instructed to remove my wet shirt. Grabbing the dripping garment from my hand, Papa passed it to Juan with the instructions to have it washed and ironed. Then, taking the tired towel I dried off and completed my task by putting on Papa's white guyabera that covered me like a circus tent.

Leaving the front hall, Hemingway directed me to follow him into what may be termed a "family/living" room. Upon entering I was a somewhat surprised by its decor. On several of the walls were two canvases by Roberto Domingo and a reproduction of the "Don Manuel Osorio Manrique de Zuniga" by Goya. On another wall was a brown stag, a trophy resulting from a hunting trip in Wyoming. Further, the walls contained book cases who's shelves held works such as: A ROOM ON THE ROUTE, BROWN'S NAUTICAL ALMANAC, THE TIMELESS LAND, THE YEARLING, THE MARCH OF A NATION, THE BOBWHITE QUAIL, PHOTOGRAPH HISTORY OF THE CIVIL WAR, etc. along with a number of Papa's works translated into foreign languages. Later, Hemingway was to inform me that at any one time La Finca held "around 7000 books."

In one corner of the room was an old Capehart record player which, so Papa said, was served by a collection of approximately 1000 records representing a varied taste: the music of the Navaho and Sioux Indians, Beethoven, Cole Porter, Bach, Eddie de Lange, Jerome Kern, the songs of the International Brigade, Brahms, beguines from Martinique, Manuel de Falla, etc. Between two armchairs was what may be called a bar-table that contained: Gordon's Gin, Old Grand Dad bourbon, Campari, Bacardi rum, White Horse scotch, Picard vermouth, Early Times, etc. The balance of the room's furniture and items was a reflection and representations of the man who had occupied it since the late 1930's -- colorful, engaging, robust, intriguing, fascinating, sincere, and realistic.

Casting a glance towards one of the two large arm chairs separated by the bar- table Papa directed, "Take a seat!"

Settling comfortably in the chair I made a few feeble comments regarding the large number of books and records when Hemingway announced, "Looks like you could use a drink! Wadda ya want?"

"A beer will be fine." I responded. "Don't think I have any -- at least not cold," Papa declared, "but you look like a man let me get ya a man's drink."

From his armchair, which was exactly as mine, with only the bar-table separating us, Papa reached across with his arm and grabbed the neck of the Old Grand bottle of bourbon on the bar-table and proceeded to fill an 8ounce glass tumbler within a fraction of an inch from the top with the amber liquid. Carefully handing me the tumbler Papa assured me, "this will get the chill out of your bones!"

As I cautiously took the glass from Papa's hand I noted by my Timex watch that it was but 9:33 a.m.! As I slowly sipped my "body warmer" Hemingway began the preliminary questions of an initial acquaintanceship.

"How long have I been in Havana? What I was doing in Cuba? Where I was staying? etc.

With the rudimentary conversation over, and I, ever so slowly sipping my "bodywarmer," Hemingway asked, "Where ya originally from?"

I leaned back in my armchair and offered, "Well, I was born in New Jersey, but I spent a lot of time in Florida."

"Where in Florida?" Papa pressed.

"The Tampa Bay area." I answered.

"That's a good area. My father use to own some property in St. Petersburg in Pinellas County but lost it after the land boom went belly up. There use to be a ferry that ran from St. Pete to Pass A Grill Beach; was a nice trip," Hemingway commented.

Hemingway reflected for a few seconds and continued with, "I use to drive through that western section of Florida on my way down to the Keys; or, coming up from the Keys on my way to Arkansas. I would stop for ice cream at a place called Webb's City that billed themselves as the "World's Most Unusual Drugstore." I used to take a car ferry called the MISS PINELLAS from Pinellas Point in St. Petersburg, south across Tampa Bay to Manatee County where I would pick up Route 41 and drive down to Sarasota. There was a great restaurant in Sarasota, right on Route 41, called THE GOLDEN BUDDA. Swell food! Jesus, that Tampa Bay area was a wonderful place for flat and bay fishing! While I would wait for the ferry to make it's round trip from Pinellas to Manatee I would visit a fishing camp a little to the west of the ferries staging area called O'Neil's run by two brothers, Grant and Howard. Late one afternoon I met this guy named Eddie Szadowsky who had caught the biggest damn speckled trout I ever saw! Some of the locals around O'Neil's figured it was going to be a bay area record. Waiting for the ferry I spent some time talking to this guy Eddie and looking at his fishing stuff. Jesus, the guy had a hell of an assortment of flat and bay gear; all good stuff: Phlugher, Ocean City, Penn reels, Barracuda Brand plugs, spoons, jigs, and trolling feathers. Christ, he was one of the most knowledgeable and best damn flat and bay fisherman I ever met! He made his own poles using hickory for the stock, bamboo for the pole, and did his own mounting for the eyes and sealed wrappings. He told me Barracuda Brands manufactured their stuff right in St. Petersburg. Maybe you know or saw the guy? Hold on a minute!" Hemingway quickly raised himself from the armchair and walked over to a table near to where the Capehart record player was located. Atop the table was a large box from which Papa retrieved several photographs. With photos in hand he walked over to where I was seated -- still sipping my "body warmer" and beginning to feel a bit warm myself -- and handed me the photographs with the instructions, "Take these. I took the photos of Eddie's speckled trout because no one else there had a camera. I told Eddie I would send the pictures to him, but I can't locate his address. You live in the Tampa Bay area. Drop them by O'Neil's." I put the photos in the shirt pocket of Papa's guyabera. Sadly, with the passing of the years I was unable to connect with Eddie Szadowsky to present him with the photos of his prized speckled trout that Hemingway had taken.

Eddie Szadowsky and his Speckled Trout

As I worked towards the bottom of my "body warmer" tumbler with about 2 ounces of the OLD GRAND DAD remaining, Hemingway asked if I did much fishing, and if I did, what type. I replied that my fishing was limited to flat and bay fishing and clearly not the "bill" type big game fishing that Hemingway was world famous for. This response did not appear to register a compliment or satisfy Papa. To the contrary, his warm encompassing eyes focused on me and he inquired more specifically with, "What do you use for gear?"

"A friend of mine has a flat bottom wooden boat with built in live bait wells. It's powered by an adequate SEA KING outboard." I remarked.

Hemingway moved his head slightly to one side and shot back with, "Hell I didn't ask you about the vessel. I asked you about your gear -- fishing gear!"

I had learned my first lesson when engaging in dialogue with Hemingway: Be certain you understand the question before you answer, and then answer specifically.

Replying as if I had not received an instruction I responded with, "I use a six foot hollow fiberglass Shakespeare rod with an aluminum stock covered over with cork. Also, I use a level winding Shakespeare reel with a 15 lb. monofilament line."

"Ya, and… "Papa remarked wanting more. I continued with,

"At the end of the line I use a double swivel with a twisted stainless steel leader that at its base is connected to another swivel with a "pelican" clamp. To this I affix a #5 shacked hook. When casing and reeling in I use 1/4 ounce lead split shot for weight."

"And for bait?" Hemingway persisted.

"I use live minnows or bay shrimp, but first I always sharpen the hook with a wet stone," I replied.

"Ya," Papa again commented this time with his head and chest moving forward, "but how do ya hook 'em?"

"The shrimp I hook either through the back or the head depending on their size and the minnows through their gills so they stay alive and can swim, I offered.

For a second Hemingway stared intensely at me -- eye to eye -- then relaxed back in his armchair and granted, "You've done some bay fishing.

I took those begrudging words to mean that I had received a reprieve from "the old man and the sea." However, my pardon was of short duration.

Continuing on with the topic of fishing I commented that in recent years the Tampa Bay area was rapidly becoming popular for spear fishing and was Cuba experiencing a similar popularity, and what did he, Hemingway, have as an opinion on spear fishing.

Hemingway instantly stated, in a raised voice, that spear fishing was NOT popular in Cuba," ... hoped to Christ it never would be!" and immediately initiated an attack on the practice of spear fishing by defining it not as a sport but as a fraud. Papa went on to accuse the very act of spearing a fish as cowardly, deceitful, and repugnant to true sportsmen. "Spear fishing participants lacked ingenuity, resourcefulness, and collectively weren't worth the powder to blow them to hell. The fish accepts with honesty and innocence a submerged person as but another creature of the sea only to have that honesty and innocence betrayed and met with impalement by a spear!

Before I could respond Papa stated, "Look, I don't want to get black ass about this!" Then leaning forward in his armchair he explained his philosophy on the sport of fishing, which synthesized, is as follows: When a rod and reel are used, the only item separating the fish from life or death is the line -- and the skill of the angler with the line. Further, when hooked, the fish knows instinctively that the hook is abnormal and will match all of its abilities and instincts for survival against the angler to gain its freedom. Consequently, for both the fish and angler, this is a supreme ordeal -- a relentless, agonizing battle with only a line separating the two combatants.

"And the spear fisherman?" I asked Papa.

"The son of a bitch is a con artist, a phony practicing marine slaughter and butchery!" proclaimed Hemingway, as he now became a bit more visceral. "Like I said before," Papa continued, "I don't want to get black ass about this, but I know fishing and I understand what is equality between two combatants. And sure as dog shit spear fishing is not equality for the fish!"

I became aware that the term "*getting black ass*" which Hemingway used periodically was equitably to one "getting pissed off."

Sagacity suggested I exit from the topic of spear fishing. Still, moving forward as a "complete angler," I asked Hemingway if, in his Upper Peninsula Michigan fishing days if he had utilized any type of watercraft. He responded with "No", that most of the fishing he did was fly casting fishing and this he did from the edges of rivers, lake shores, or piers. Next, I confidently stated that his PILAR was without doubt the most renowned and noted vessel in the Gulf of Mexico, Florida Straits, and Florida Atlantic Coast. In response to this statement, Hemingway's face beamed and, recovering a bit of composure he commented that indeed he had put "quite a few hours on the engines of the PILAR."

Having lived near the sea all my life and participated for most of that time in the sport of fishing, I was fully cognizant that it was unthinkable for any self-respecting fisherman to practice his sport on a boat that did not belong to him. This maxim was patently true as applied to Hemingway. Thus, I quickly followed up by inquiring of Papa as to when he secured the PILAR, from who, what were the vessels appointments and specifications, and to what extent did Papa have a hand in any modifications that may have been made. Observing that my "body warming" glass was now almost empty, Hemingway started to raise from his armchair at the same time inquiring as to if I wished a refill. Smiling, I assured him I did not -- at least not at this time.

Relaxing in his armchair Papa related as to how when he lived in Key West a friend told him about a boat builder in New York City, New York -- Wheeler Shipyard, who had a reputation for building "meat and potato" fishing vessels that were sound, reliable, and functional; void of all the "glitter, bells, horns, and whistles" found on many so called fishing water craft. Subsequently, Papa continued, once he saw his way clear financially he placed an order for the boat based on what he believed has needs would be for "bill fishing" and took some guidance from some "fishing pals -- all swell guys" in Key West. This was in 1934. I asked Papa if he had taken delivery of the vessel in New York City and was told no; that the boat had been shipped by train to Miami where delivery was taken from Miami whereupon Papa and a friend had then transported the vessel to Key West where he kept it at the naval station.

Having salt water in my veins and in later years would come to own my own charter boat business, I questioned Hemingway regarding the PILAR's specifications. Papa pressed himself against the back of his armchair, titled his head slightly to one side as I would observe to be a habit of his, developed a pensive expression, and began to expound: The wooden material used for the construction of the PILAR was dark oak. Her LWL (length water line) dimension was 38 feet with bow to stem measuring 42 feet. She had twin screws with double rudders and was powered by diesels. The PILAR's cruising range was approximately 500 miles -- given the variables associated with wind, drift, and current. For accommodations, Hemingway continued without missing a beat, the PILAR had three separate compartments under the fore-deck with one cabin/galley and two double berths providing ample space for six to eight passengers. Operationally, the PILAR carried 300 gallons of diesel and 150 gallons of water in her tanks. It could carry a further 200 gallons of water in drums along with a ton of ice. As I listened attentively to Hemingway itemize the specifics that comprised the PILAR I became in awe of Papa's enormous capacity for facts, figures, data, information, minute details and nuances. This capacity I would come to witness as Hemingway demonstrated the same ability with virtually all topics and subjects, directly or indirectly.

Moving forward, Hemingway continued to retrieve from his mind additional specifics concerning the PILAR. One of the three separate compartments under the fore-deck containing the two double berths had built-in drawers beneath the lower bunk, two closets and a small table. The second compartment contained the galley and the head. The third compartment contained another double berth and two open shelves. Drawing a deep breath, Papa detailed that forward of the helm was the console that contained four marine gauges: two served as monitors for the engine oil and temperature of the engines, the other two were a tachometer to indicate the engines RPM's. To the left of the console was a marine board with vertical switches for the ground tackle-light, running lights, bilge pump, and search light. Enough, I thought of the specifications and injected the question as to how the vessel came to be called the PILAR. Hemingway stated that his floating sanctuary was named in honor of the shrine and the feria at Zaragoza, Spain.

Attempting some humor I inquired of Papa if aboard the PILAR and when the vessel is underway if he were an archetype of Captain Bliegh. Smiling, Hemingway made it lucid that a sad mistake made by many would be mariners who owned sea craft was that of attempting to be: captain, helmsmen, and navigator. Always, Papa lectured, "responsibility must be delegated to competent sea proven personal -- and if the bastards aren't competent and sea proven don't let them aboard. Remember the old adage that "... one servant does not serve two masters equally well."

"Okay, when you're at sea and attempting to serve to three masters --captain, helmsmen, and navigator you're only diluting your own effectiveness and efficiency as owner of the vessel and placing all who are participating in the sea voyage in danger!"

In later years when I served as foredecks men and medial personal aboard a 10 meter sailing vessel racing biannually from Marion, Massachusetts to Bermuda this same rational was succinctly focused on as a safety factor to be incorporated in the racing/sailing plan of each participant who undertook the Bermuda Sailing Race passage.

With me having Papa acknowledge that he relinquished his "captains seat" I pursued the next and obvious question, "Who is the captain of the PILAR?"

Hemingway stated that Gregorio Fuentes is, and has been, the captain of the PILAR for "a long time" and is assisted by Anselmo Hernandez whenever the PILAR was underway for a "bill" fishing voyage. Moreover, Hemingway continued as to how Gregorio Fuentes had a full and clear understanding of "El Corriente del Golfo," (the Gulf Stream). A good fisherman knows that the corriente flows only about 350 yards north of El Morro, and how the fisherman would know how to easily distinguish the current. Further, Papa stated that "Captain Fuentes" knew the surface of the Gulf Stream is a much deeper blue than the water that lies on either side and that it is this contrasting color which indicates that the waters are quite different in nature and temperature. Now, Papa spoke more intensely and began to lean forward a little from his armchair as he related how dozens of generations of Cuban fisherman before Gregorio Fuentes had called the demarcation line between the two blues the "hilero." And being a descendent from these generations of fisherman Gregorio Fuentes knew all the good spots for fishing, the places where he would have the best chance to catch the biggest fish. Papa now more relaxed then the heretofore intensity displayed began to speak in an almost eulogistic manner as he shared with me how Gregorio Fuentes had studied the movements of the corriente. Also, he knew that it originated to the southwest of Cuba, off Cape San Antonio and then follows the northern coast of the island, after which it flows up past Key West, Miami and Cape Hatteras before turning in a north easterly direction towards Europe and the Canary Islands. Too, Captain Fuentes understood that another current, known as the North Equatorial Current, then swept down, past the Canaries and across the Atlantic again towards the Caribbean and Yucatan in Mexico to complete an enormous circle. Papa continued that Gregorio comprehended how the Gulf Stream flowed nearest to Havana in an easterly direction, that it was 60 miles wide at that particular point, and that its speed depended on its depth, varying between 1.5 and 2.5 knots off Havana.

Hemingway never missed a beat with his reportage that now developed a rhythm as he elaborated about how Captain Fuentes understood the migratory habits of the spearfish and their feeding habits and how it is to the "hilero" that the really big fish come to feed and if one opened the stomach of a marlin to examine the contents, how one would find every variety of small fish that lives just on the edge of the corriente. Gregorio knew the spearfish migrate from west to east, but are easier to catch when swimming in the opposite direction, just outside the corriente, when they venture in search of food. He knew the blue marlin arrived from April to May in this zone, but it is only from September onwards that you can catch the really big ones, the "heavyweights," as Papa called them.

"And if you're out in the corriente and it's too late to head back to the PILAR's home port of Cojimar (approximately 12 miles north of La Finca)?" I asked.

"Not to worry," Papa assured. Cojimar, a small fishing village and home port of the PILAR was not the only "resting spot" for as Hemingway affirmed, "Captain Gregorio knows plenty of them," For example, Papa noted, there is Mariel, Bahia Blanca, and Jijira between the ports of Juraco and Santa Cruz -- all well sheltered harbors that can serve well as a temporary base of operation and provide good over night anchorage.

Next, I refocused my question again to that of the PILAR's specifications and inquired of Hemingway as to if he was involved in any design modifications of the vessel. Papa grinned and acknowledged that the fly bridge was the only modification he allowed himself as it offered a clearer view of fishing activities. Upon Hemingway completing his remarks regarding the fly bridge there existed one of those rare few seconds of silence and at that instance our eyes met and a feeling of euphoria with a dash of intimidation rushed through me. At this juncture I ventured into deep waters by offering my philosophical interpretation of Papa's curriculum vitae of Gregorio's lifelong affair with "El Corriente del Golfo." As our eyes remained fixed -- Hemingway's more transfixed than mine, I managed to mumble something that approximated "From the nautical resume of Captain Fuentes, (my attempt to inject a bit of jocularity), you've got a great deal of admiration for the captain's knowledge, ability, and experience.

Oh, hell, yes Shadow! Damn right! I respect him!!! Hemingway always called me "Shadow," never Roger, and I never learned why.

As a point of fact Hemingway loved Gregorio Fuentes and validation of this was demonstrated later in the day when Papa told me that when he made out his will in the early 1950's he left the PILAR to Captain Fuentes. I shifted the next inquiry to tournaments and told Hemingway that I was aware of The Annual Hemingway Marlin-Fishing Competition that began in 1950 and did he enjoy and participate. Papa developed a frown and retorted with, "Hell no! Most of the "players" are a bunch of drunks with too much time too much money and know too little about sea craft and fishing! I let them use my name -- nothing more!

With the hours slipping by and Papa showing a greater measure of relaxation and I becoming more confident with my questions, dialogue, and repartee I synthesized the more salient segments of our conversation which encouraged me to conclude that for Papa fishing had long ago ceased to be a game or sport. True, when Hemingway initially discovered big-game fishing in Key West through his pal Josie Russell it became his abiding passion, and a recurrent theme in his later writings. True, from the onset of his early participation in the sport of "bill" fishing he learned quickly and soon acquired a formidable reputation; especially as relates to his technique of struggling with his prey and pulling it in as quickly as possible so that the sharks could not take bites out of it made Papa an overnight celebrity in fishing circles. Now, however, when Hemingway spoke about the "water being fished-out" in recent years there was an undercurrent of frustration and anger in his tone. And what about those times when Hemingway and Captain Fuentes embarked upon "El Corrients del Golfo" from Cojimar only to return with no "heavyweights"? Only a true fisherman can hope to understand Hemingway's reaction on these particular occasions for he took such events as a wound to his pride, and, although every true fisherman who ever lived has experienced that feeling of injured pride when the fish just aren't there; in Hemingway the feeling took on colossal proportions. Moreover, to exasperate those times, especially when others were aboard, Papa would provide sufficient blame to go around. To this end, every activity connected with big-game fishing was looked upon as a ritual and had to be carried out according to strict rules. And God protect anyone who dared break those rules from Hemingway's wrath! As a result, Papa was as obsessed by the "hilero" and what it contained as he was obsessed by the City of Paris or by the slopes of Mt. Kilimanjaro in Africa.

40

As if established by a predetermined cue, Papa burst forth with, "Ya hungry?"

"Ya sure." I answered not certain if the early morning rising, the sub conscience anxiety of my discussions with Papa, or the slow nursing of my now empty glass of "body warmer" had generated my appetite.

"Lety! Lety! Pase por un momentito por favor," Papa bellowed from his armchair. In a moment a short, copper-skinned woman with long black hair, dark eyes, full lips, and a gentle smile entered the living room, stood near Hemingway and responded with,

"Digome."

Hemingway replied with, "Tu conoce el menu. Queremos almorzamos.

"Si," Lety acknowledged, "Al instante." And she departed.

"We'll eat in a few minutes," Papa proclaimed, and then with piercing eyes beholding my empty glass inquired, "Ya ready for another drink?"

"Not quite yet," I offered and followed up with,

"Aren't you gonna have one?"

"Don't drink in the mornings when I have a work schedule," Hemingway managed in a low voice.

In a few moments Lety entered and with her infectious smile proclaimed, "Almuerzoes lista!"

"Let's go! Hemingway beckoned with his right hand.

I rose first from my armchair and as I did so viewed a portrait of Hemingway that was clearly done years ago. As I continued to gaze upon the work -- especially the unique hairstyle sported by Papa I felt Hemingway's eyes upon me. I turned and looked at Papa whereupon he remarked, "That was done by an old friend, Waldo Peirce who was a friend of the journalist Jack Reed. Mrs. Mary likes it, but this is one of my favorites," and Hemingway motioned with his left hand to a painting by the Spanish master, Juan Gris.

In response I confessed to but a rudimentary knowledge of paintings, and said no more. As Papa and I left the 50 foot living room we turned into the foyer of La Finca with its view into the dining room. To the left were more mountings of game secured from hunting expeditions and a large magazine rack that contained journals, periodicals, publications, etc. from all over the world and in a variety of different languages. With the entering of the dining room

I noted another small room that extended beyond and which had double doors opening to the outside of the building. Again, there were two mountings of what appeared to be antelope heads. As I walked on the red-brown tile floor of the dining room towards the charming table, Hemingway motioned with his hand and directed me to, "Grab a seat!"

Mindful of good decorum I deferred taking a chair at the end of the table and selected one in the middle. Hemingway took a chair directly across for me. Almost instantly, except for Hemingway and I, the solitariness in this beautiful dining room became pronounced and subsequently I understood why. Hemingway was looking to his left through the double doors of the small room at some outside distraction.

I asked, "Will Mrs. Mary be joining us?"

"No. She left last night to spend a few days in Havana with some friends," Hemingway replied, never taking his now narrowed and focused eyes off the outside distraction. Accordingly, while Papa continued to be momentarily occupied I began looking more closely at two beautiful contemporary reflecting lamps which adorned the dining table and which I had admired when we first came into to room. So as to inspect one of the lamps more closely I reached with my right hand to pick one up when Hemingway, no longer distracted, turned, looked at me, and warned, "Shadow, if you don't want to see someone get "black ass" fast be goddamn careful with those lamps! Mrs. Mary got 'em in France and she loves 'em!"

Smiling, I looked at Papa, with drew my hand, and stated, "I hear you. Also, I have never been accused of having dexterous fingers."

While awaiting the arrival of lunch, Juan Pastor came in with a large carafe, two glasses, and placed them in the center of the table, whereupon Papa announced, "Got some good red table wine -- want some?"

My inclination was to acknowledge in the affirmative. Still, a measure of my better judgment obligated me to remind Hemingway about my glass of OLD GRAND DAD.

"Christ, I told you that you look like a man!" Hemingway asserted and concluded with, Ya should be able to handle a couple of glasses of red table wine!"

"I don't drink alone, and you said you don't drink when you're working," I countered.

42

"Ya didn't listen Shadow!" Papa stated and then proclaimed, "I said I don't drink in the MORNING when I have a work schedule! Hell, its 12:45!

"All right," I chuckled, "I'll have some."

"Help yourself! Take the carafe!" Hemingway instructed.

We both filled our glasses, raised them, exchanged glances, and drank. The wine was dry, yet not sharp or acid, free of sediment, and had a pleasant bouquet.

"From Spain?" I implored Hemingway.

"Don't know," Papa confessed. "The kitchen gets it here in the pueblo when they do their shopping. They say it comes in bulk from Havana." Papa continued.

After the passing of a few moments Lety came into the dining room with a large wooden tray, placed it on a stationary serving table, disappeared, and as quickly reappeared with yet another large wooden tray. The spicy aroma drifting from the food was marvelous! Clearly, I was hungrier than I thought. As Lety began placing the culinary delights from the serving table onto the dining table, Papa issued the command, "Dig in!"

Taking another swallow of the now delightful red table wine that was becoming more agreeable; I reviewed the options that were before me. The trays held a plate of fresh sliced avocado, a sauce dish containing minced garlic, lime juice and ground pepper, a bamboo basket with fresh "pan Cubano" (Cuban bread). A large bowl was filled with "arroz amarillo con frijoles negro y cebolla" (yellow rice with black beans and onion), and a large platter of "pollo asado" (roasted-- not fried -- chicken). While devouring my delicious "bill of fare", I noticed on the table ware a most unique design and inquired of Hemingway as to its significance; whereupon he elucidated: It was the emblem of La Finca Vigia. Specifically, the symbol at the top represents the three "mountains" of Paris -- Montparnasse, Montmartre, and the Montagne Sainte-Genevieve- ----as well as the three hills of La Finca Vigia. The arrowhead below was borrowed from the Ojibwa tribe, whose territory covered the north of Michigan and Minnesota, where Papa related he spent a lot of his time in his youth. Likewise, the horizontal strips at the bottom represent the rank of captain awarded both to Mrs. Mary and Papa during the Second World War. Finishing my last slice of avocado with large amounts of the lime/garlic sauce followed by the final fork full of yellow rice and black beans, I automatically reached for the new almost empty carafe of red table wine and began refilling my glass.

Hemingway flashed one of his contagious smiles as he cleaned every speck of meat, skin, fat, and gristle off the chicken bones and declared, "Not bad stuff; hay Shadow!"

"Not bad stuff at all, Papa!" I agreed.

With this Papa shouted, "Juan, el otro garrafa de vino tinto, por favor!"

Shortly, the congenial Juan returned with another -- and larger -- carafe of red table wine. Hemingway leaned back in his chair and asked if I had been to any of the racing kennels, the race track, or jai alai "fontons" in Havana. When I informed him I had not Papa again called the faithful Juan, said something to him that I did not fully hear, and again leaned back in his chair awaiting Juan's return which was prompt and handed to Hemingway what looked like -- and which proved to be, a card. Leaning forward, Hemingway handed the card to me that read: GRANDSTAND, BILTMORE KENNEL CLUB, PLAYA DE MARIANO, SERVICE CHARGE 10cts. As I was examining the card Hemingway told me to forget about the grandstand and 10cts. That's when I went to the Biltmore Kennel Club I was to ask directly for the manager, a "Vincente Monterey", give the card to "Vincente," and tell him you are a friend of "Mr. Way". Continuing, Papa related that he knew "Vincente" and assured me "Vincente" would get me into the Biltmore's private club plus some free booze. Placing the card in my wallet I thanked Papa, but cast him a quizzical grin and commented, "Mr. Way!" Papa looked straight at me and confirmed, "Mr. Way"

Later, I would learn that Hemingway loved nicknames and indeed invented many of them that included, but were not limited to, Ernie, Hern, Wemedge, Dr. Heminstein, Ernest Hemorrhoid, Mr. Way, and his favorite -- Papa.

With our stomachs full, our glasses refilled, a subtle tranquility encompassed the wonderful dining room and I share with Hemingway that the Tampa Bay area boasted a jai alai facility that provided single and paired matched games. Also, I remarked I was surprised more jai alai players did not come to the Tampa Bay area from the Basque Region of Spain prior to, during, and after the Spanish Civil War given the large Spanish speaking population that Tampa has always had and the popularity of jai alai.

"It's not because they didn't want to," Hemingway somberly stated. I was cognizant of Hemingway's legendary multi-faceted participation in the Spanish Civil War as observer, journalist, narrator, and along with Dutch filmmaker Joris Ivens co-producer of the film documentary THE SPANISH EARTH. Further, this participation included Hemingway being writer, fund raiser for the Loyalist, heroic activist, and clarion who along with Lillian Hellman, James Lardner, H. G. Wells trumpeted to a deaf world the rapid arrival of fascism with their black angels of terror and death personified by Franco's Nationals with Mussolini's and Hitler's support. Also, I was fully aware of the personal and .financial role that Hemingway played in bringing many Republic Basque jai alai players to the safety of Cuba's shores; who, if Hemingway had not done so, would have with mathematical certainty, been executed by Franco forces. Consequently, all of the aforementioned served to earn for Hemingway a "badge" of hatred and detestation from Franco and the fascist -- which Papa wore with pride. Hemingway's head bent forward a bit as he looked at his plate with the fork at the center and the knife at the top and moved his right hand slowly forward towards the half filled glass of red table wine. Hunching his shoulders he drew a deep breath and without looking at me said, "Shadow, as many of the world's nations send their sons and daughters to America's shores the initial sight for these children of other lands is the weeping of a lady standing tall and proud -- and the name of the lady is the Statue of Liberty. This lady weeps out of sadness, yes, but this sadness has been induced by betrayal. The sadness rest at the ladies feet with the words, "Give Me Your Tired, Your Poor, Your Huddled Masses Yearning To Breathe Free-----".

"And the betrayal?" I asked.

Hemingway took a long, deliberate swig of the red table wine and responded with, "the betrayal, Shadow, is that the lady has been told by the politicians that America does not want the tired, poor, huddled masses of other neighbor nations and we don't give a damn if they do yearn to breathe free!"

Leaning back in his chair and with his right hand clasping the now half filled glass of red table wine, Hemingway cast me an intense gaze and continued with, "Shadow, you look like an okay guy, so understand this -- its a fact indelibly inscribed in the chronicles of our history that in its courtship of immigrants the United States has always been more interested in the courtship than the marriage -- and the wedding has only been pursued when the United States economy was in need of immigrant sweat and blood."

With a final swig, Papa emptied the glass of the charming red nectar, automatically seized the carafe and refilled his glass, as did I immediately thereafter, and moved forward with, "Serious scholars such as Henry Steele Commager, Samuel Eliot Morison, and others concur that under the epidermis of "Americana" there has always existed suspicion, prejudice, and hate of immigrants and these dog shit characteristics become our government policies whenever we are in need of deflecting our own self-generated ills from ourselves to the easy target of "foreigners" who may embrace their heritage, speak with an accent, or have skin color that is less than white. The thought is never entertained by slow-witted policy makers that it is difficult for the politicians to trust someone they do not understand with the result that immigrants are viewed through the eyes of ignorance which is through the eyes of fear. The result is humanistic values are subordinated to political ambitions and the lives of our future good friends and new neighbors destroyed with blind arrogance."

With his left hand Hemingway took some Cuban bread breaking off pieces, dipping them into the bowel of lime juice and garlic, consuming the "botanitas", and washing them down with the red table wine. I was enjoying the last of the fresh avocados while Papa continuing to eat, instructed me that, "Its bitter irony that within the historical text of the initial chapters have their pages besmirched with accounts of prejudice and hate directed towards the only true Americans -- the native American Indians! Understand, Shadow, anthropologically unless someone is a native American Indian they are not Americans, but by birth U.S. citizens; descendants from those who came mainly from Europe -- Euro-Americans -- themselves immigrants to the land of the native American Indians. Then, after these Euro-Americans secured a firm foothold on North American soil they inaugurated the dark trade of slavery-- and did so with zeal! And, I'll tell ya Shadow, this bitter irony acquired a new dimension when it was incorporated into the first official American Policy By Exclusion on July 4, 1776 with the signing of the Declaration of Independence proclaiming freedom; for, on that day over a million slaves were owned by these Euro-Americans.

46

"Get it right Shadow, when ya thumb through the text of our U.S. history ya continue to encounter malicious treatment of immigrants. Hell, no geographical section of our country can claim a monopoly on discrimination. To the contrary, intolerance was distributed demographically, democratically and proportionally to the Orientals on the West Coast, to the Mexicans in the South West, to the French Canadians to the North, to the Germans, Irish, Jews, Slavic groups, and members of the "Mediterranean Menace" represented by Greeks and Italians in the East. Jesus Christ, no immigrant to our shores has been spared!" As Papa paused to wet his whistle with the once again filled glass of red table wine, I capitalized on the moment of silence to share with him my own recollection of incidents shared with me by my grandparents who had come to America in the early 1900's and had themselves become pariahs because of their foreign culture and language thereby being subjected to much in the way of rudeness and insults.

Papa put his glass down, titled his head to the left slightly and asked, "Shadow you've seen the photo of the two railroads meeting at Promontory Point, Utah?"

I confirmed that I had.

Papa leaned back again in his chair and declared, 'There is not one poor Chinese in the goddamn photo! After busting their ass, living in hell, and dying the only people who were allowed in the photos were whites -- and most of them politicians! Did ya know that the Chinese people, including those born in America, were not given the right to vote until the early 1940's? I get real black ass about this Shadow and I'm telling ya those faces in the photo at Promontory Point says it all!"

"What is it specifically that the photo says?" I probed.

Hemingway again titled his head to the left, leaned a bit more back in his chair and stated, "One of the contributing factors involved with prejudice and hate towards immigrants rest within the reality that a distinctive quality of the "American Persona" is that of the White Anglo Saxon Protestant. Subsequently, when our government fails to put "square immigrant pegs" into its "round WASP holes," it interprets and utilizes obscure and dogmatic laws and policies by having the Immigration and Naturalization Service shave the pegs! Consequentially, for the immigrants, they are cast among the strangling weeds of bigotry and intolerance that have always grown well in our garden of freedom and justice. Papa stretched out his right arm and with his large hand grabbed the carafe of red table wine, motioned to me to put my glass under the carafe's spout, filled my glass, filled his, and called out, "Juan, Lety, otro garrafa de vino!" In a few moments Lety, with her ingratiating smile entered and placed a full carafe in the middle of the table and removed the empty one. Papa placed his arms on the table, leaned forward, and began, "I use to spend a lot of time in the late spring and summer in the U-P of Michigan (Upper Peninsula). My father had a nice cabin there and I use to do a lot of fishing, hunting, exploring, and all that good stuff that young men do. My father was a doctor, a damn good one, a sensitive man."

I acknowledged to Hemingway that I had read where his father was a physician and that he would take Hemingway to the U-P to spend the summer there. "That wasn't my point," Papa related. "My point is that our cabin was located where there were a large number of Ojibwa Indians -- dirt poor, yes, but honest, loyal and honorable. Over the years I got to know them, their customs, and learned some of their language. When members of their tribe got sick, my father would tend to their needs -- and never charged them a damn cent! But get this Shadow, in a day or two or even a week members of the tribe would show up at the cabin door -- always early in the morning with a string of fish or bowls of berries to repay what they considered a moral obligation. The message is this: these were Native Americans who retained their dignity and pride and repaid an obligation out of their understanding the VALUE of something -- not the PRICE of something -- and the repayment was to a White Angelo Saxon Protestant doctor, a Euro-American!"

Like many Americans, I was painfully aware of the United States' shameful and disgraceful treatment of Native Americans. Still, I elected not to reenact the battle of the Little Big Horn with Papa; but in lieu of engaging in dialogue on the historical maltreatment of Native Americans I opted to revisit a statement Hemingway had earlier made.

As I sipped my red table wine, I moved to mention to Hemingway, "Papa, you used a phrase before, "American Policy By Exclusion," can you clarify that for me.

Hemingway flashed his wide grin and offered, "Shit yes! I'll give you two examples, but understand they are not isolated incidents but are representative of a consistent ongoing pattern of aberrations that has been and continues to remain with us. First, in 1938 the approximately 1,000 passengers aboard the vessel ST. LOUIS of the Hamburg-Amerika Line, in a desperate effort to receive sanctuary from the purity of horror as personified in the form of fascist concentration camps, were, after undergoing a voyage of anxiety, eventually returned to the terror from which they were frantically fleeing -- victims of our governments anti-immigration and anti-Semitic policies. Specifically, the U.S. Department of State, the U.S. Justice Department, and the INS had chosen to enforce a rigid and archaic quota system for accepting immigrants. Our government officials and politicians didn't give a rats ass that the passengers had their U.S. papers in order, that they possessed U.S. immigration numbers which would become meaningless if the passengers were returned to Nazi Germany. In the eyes of our government these "foreigners" would "-----just have to wait their turn." This was bullshit! Of the hundreds of passengers; men, woman and children who were sent to concentration camps as a result of our government's policy only a handful survived the gas chamber. Those poor wretched souls partook of a voyage that made an exit from insanity to an open door of freedom that our government silently shut in their faces.

As Hemingway took another gulp of wine I injected the question, "Wasn't there anyone in Washington in '38 to stand up and shout, "Stop! This is wrong!"

"Sure, a few people," Papa acknowledged, "but ya gotta remember this in politics Shadow it takes more courage to do what is right than to do what is wrong, and as our politicians should have learned from their contemporary Herr Doctor Goebbels, sometimes a great lie is easier to believe than a great truth-- but it doesn't mean that the truth is any less a fact -- and the fact remained that anti-immigration and anti-Semitism was -- and is -- the "coin of the realm" with our government's policies of exclusion. Jesus Christ, Shadow, think back and you'll remember that after the horror of the ST. LOUIS incident our government's policies of prejudice against all "foreign type people" demonstrated its own capacity to inaugurate a variation of concentration camps when Washington put a fancy phrase on such facilities by euphemistically referring to them as "relocation centers". This policy had added to it a new twist that was to have far more deadly consequences by including the expression of justification for such actions as being done '--in the interest of National Security.' Then, into these 'centers' thousands of loyal, honest Japanese were herded, torn from their homes in this, the land of the free, by our government and placed behind barbed wire. When released from these houses of humiliation they were provided with a government quip that equated to, "Dreadfully sorry, all a terrible misunderstanding." When it comes to immigrants, Shadow, the bottom line is that our government places intolerance inside bigotry and wraps it in an agenda for policies."

In defense of my patriotism I pulled myself up in my chair, took a large swallow of wine, looked directly at Hemingway, and stated, "Papa, I understand that the tired eyes of a troubled world looks upon America's treatment of immigrants and ask "Why?" Still, I'm sure you'll agree that there are many nations who respond to immigrants, or those who cross their boarders, or are politically relocated in a far more draconian manner than the United States does."

"Well hell, yes," Papa stated, "and I'll tell who a bunch of them are: Spain, Mainland China, a lot of the African Nations, the collective Soviet Union and its satellites, and a shit pot full of the Arab countries! Nevertheless, unlike we in the United States those nations who violate human rights -- or worst are oblivious to the reality that they even exist -- don't circumnavigate the globe instructing the world to practice freedom and democracy and boastfully bellowing that in so doing they can attain 'wealth' and 'power.'" Now, leaning forward, Papa narrowed his eyes and with a smile concluded "On the contrary, we Americans have been wisely instructed by our sister and brother nations to practice more of what we preach and preach less of what we practice and told there is a differential between "wealth" and excellence and "power" and greatness. Myself, I simply choose to recognize that the fact is, America is here because immigrants were there and that inclusion as a policy -- not exclusion is the key to our survival as a great nation. Immigration policies and laws may determine what rights are -- not what justice is."

I leaned back in my chair and remarked, "If I hear you correctly, then you're saying that the law controls what immigrants can do -- not what they think."

"To some degree" Hemingway commented. He continued with, "Look, the United States is moving into a world defined by technology and market forces. To participate effectively and economically we are required to change. But, change can came from the power of great diversity; however, only change that has redeeming qualities can come when that diversity units to from the power of one. America can not allow its participation to become ineffective through the dilution of malice towards immigrants."

"Like the Japanese and Jews," I stated.

"Like the Japanese and Jews and any 'foreign looking' person! Hell, even the damn krauts were hustled into the so called relocation centers!" Papa confirmed.

"You mean the German prisoners of war?" I asked.

"Shit no Shadow!" Hemingway bellowed. "I mean Germans who immigrated here before the Second World War or, in some cases, who were born here and whose parents had immigrated to the U.S."

Expressing surprise, I blurted, "Where in the hell were these centers? How many of them were there?"

"There were over a dozen and I think the largest one was located in Crystal City, Texas; but hell, the inmates represented no danger even if a few were sympathetic to National Socialism," Hemingway related.

"I don't want to drive a tack with a sledge hammer on this immigration thing, but how does our government manage to execute policies of disaffection and exclusion with the eyes of the collective media scrutinizing its actions?" I inquired.

As Hemingway was about to launch into an oration, Lety came into the dining room wearing her wonderful smile and began clearing the table whereupon Papa grinned and instructed her to bring yet another carafe of the 'jolly" red table wine. With the table clearing task completed and our glasses again filled, Hemingway tightened his lips, then carefully took a deep breath and stated, "Any legislator and policy maker knows it's easier to believe a lie than the truth and our government's legislators and policy makers are no different than any others. Understanding this, legislators give their efforts and energies caring more about what is popular than what is the truth. From this baseline everything that legislators do is calculated for media effect. Therefore, when our laws and policies become non-productive is resolving our socioeconomic ills then as a nation we begin to experience frustration, insecurities and uncertainties about the future. When this happens, what do the politicians do to protect themselves?"

"They, and some select media institutions, give the people a scapegoat," I responded.

"Ya lined that one up right, Shadow, with the result that many of our laws and policies regarding immigration is bad by design and a disaster by default. Now get this, Shadow, the mind of man only knows the world that it understands therefore the more we know about one another the greater our chance of resolving internal and external conflicts. With this whole question of immigrants, the U.S. has, and continues, embarking upon a hazardous voyage in troubled-waters that has disturbing currents -- and I don't see the storm passing quickly. Ya know immigrants have been told that Americans are a fair and impartial people. What immigrants don't understand is that applies only when the mood suits Americans. Did ya know Shadow that in 1942 FDR requested of Congress a bill to ease restrictions for immigrants to enter the U.S.?"

I confessed that I did not.

Papa continued with, "Congress killed the bill which effectively killed thousands of would be immigrants -- many of them Jews. Even the media was unvarnished in their reporting that anti-Semitism in Congress killed the bill. Then, like now, most legislators don't have the courage of loyalty to humanity, only the conviction of their vanity in office. They love to provide and give the tender mercies of their injustice. I've always believed that those bastards who deny freedom to others don't deserve any for themselves. Hell, for politicians the cure for all social problems is 'law and order' enforced by a strong man! Christ, if historically America had stopped immigration, then all that we in the U.S. have been would never be!"

Hemingway's assessment of America's continued cruel enactment of prejudicial policies towards immigrants has proven accurate. Future years witnessed the U.S. Justice Dept. via INS creating clandestine task forces to specifically target immigrants. One of these is entitled The Alien Boarder Control Committee that employees the use of terror against specific groups of immigrants who, at a particular time frame, are not popular or 'politically correct' much like segments of the infamous 'Nuremberg Laws.'

Likewise, the mid 1990's witnessed President Clinton signing legislation that allows immigrants to be arrested, detained, languish in jails, and deported without due process. And, after the barbaric and horrific events of September 11, 2001 emotions surpassed wisdom with the targeting of people from the Middle East with added the added support and governmental approval of 'racial profiling,' a ludicrous tactic developed from an art to a science by the Third Reich. Excusing myself I rose from my most comfortable chair -- and made more comfortable by the 'jolly; red table wine -- and made my way to the bathroom with its walls covered with notations and numbers written mostly in pencil. In addition, there were bottles, jars, containers, tubes, vials, and boxes containing salves, ointments, pills, and liquids scattered about. I understood that Hemingway was prone to high blood pressure and high cholesterol and no doubt took medication for each. Still, the amount of pharmaceuticals in the bathroom was awesome. Returning to the dining room Hemingway was again looking through the windows of the doors that led to the outside at the distraction that had heretofore caught his attention.

Observing me entering the dining area and just as I was about to sit down, Papa asked, "Wanna take a walk around the place?"

Glancing at my Timex watch I noted that it was late in the afternoon and that time had vanished as Hemingway and I were visiting many islands in the stream of life. "Sure," I said.

As I followed Hemingway out of the dining room, Papa went over to a corner of the hallway and secured a large cudgel that was something between a big Black Forest walking stick and a pub keepers shillelagh. "For prowlers," Papa said with a grin.

"Oh," I stated, "I thought perhaps I had pissed you off."

No response from Papa. Again, my attempt at jocularity bombed.

Walking out the front entrance from whence I had entered in the morning I became aware that immediately in front of La Finca was a giant ceiba tree with orchids growing from its gnarled trunk and its massive roots up heaving the tiled terrace and indeed splitting the interior of the Finca itself Because of the morning rain I failed to take notice of this when I arrived. Now, I commented to Hemingway that perhaps the roots of the tree needed cutting; or maybe the tree itself removed.

Papa stopped, looked at the tree, then me, and threatened, "If any son of a bitch goes near this old friend with as much as a pen knife I'll bash the bastard's head in!"

As we started down the terrace steps, I, again, cautiously stepping around the piles of animal droppings, Papa charging forth with cudgel in hand and stepping on the piles with his brown loafers. Walking together I asked Hemingway when he acquired La Finca Vigia.

Looking straight ahead Papa related, "Well, first I rented it. Then in 1940 I bought it through a realtor who my former wife was steered to by the wife of a contact at Pan American Airlines." Hemingway was referring to Martha Gellhorn who was the third of Papa's four wives and who had contact with Jane Mason, wife of G. Grant Mason, then head of Pan American Airways in Cuba.

Continuing in our direction to the left I followed through on my initial question and asked, "As a matter of interest Papa, how much did La Finca cost?"

Hemingway, with his unvaried focus straight ahead and never breaking his steady stride allowed, with another of his famous grins, "Over 10 grand, less than 20."

It was now approaching dusk and as the tropical sun was gently slipping into the breast of the Gulf of Mexico for yet another night it splashed gracefully its cheerful hues and tones of orange, red, and yellow against the western sky. Hemingway assured me that given the elevation of La Finca and the brisk, cool northeast breeze we would not be besieged by mosquitoes; and, as we walked he slowed his pace pausing and stopping periodically to handle and play with the cats that were in abundance at La Finca. I inquired as to where all the cats came from and about how many of them there were.

Hemingway said that most of the cats," ... came from the Village of San Francisco," and that there "-----might be about 50 cats." On our stroll was a dark brownish dog of an indeterminable breed who Papa frolicked with and called appropriately, "Brownie." When I asked Papa about Brownie he stated that the dog had been around for a long time, was a gift from a villager, and, so stated Papa was, "a great pal and a swell dog." Picking Brownie up and hugging him, Papa flashed a big satisfied smile. With the cats behind us, many with bizarre names that Hemingway gave them including, but not limited to, "Mister Puss Nose", "Little Red", "Oreo", "Howie", "Peppers", "Bella", "Gretta", "Smokey", "Otis"... etc. we came upon an enclosure. It was here, Papa explained, that he kept his fighting cocks and asked if I had seen a cock fight ending with the statement that cock fighting was a "bloody beauty of a sport." I confirmed to Papa that I had not seen a cock fight and was glad that he did not pursue the inquiry any further as the concept of cock fighting held no interest for me. At this point a young black man came up to Hemingway and he was introduced to me as Rene Villarreal, the house servant.

Coming around the back side of La Finca I spotted a cottage that Hemingway said was La Finca's guest house and to which later Rene would take me. Curiosity seizing me I inquired, "Papa, how old is La Finca and what's its relation to San Francisco de Paula?"

Hemingway related that the Village of San Francisco de Paula grew up around a hermitage, built in the eighteenth century by a colonist from the Canaries called Augustine de Arocha. In the nineteenth century the Spanish army installed an observation post on this site, providing the name -- La Vigia, the lookout -- and the foundations for La Finca Vigia -- The Lookout Farm. Papa continued that in lieu of the village of San Francisco de Paula being poverty stricken he loved the uneven terrain of La Finca, with a hill to the north, where the narrow Rio Luyano flows and the fact that La Finca is approximately a 25 minute ride to Havana and approximately 11 miles from the sea. Further, Hemingway acknowledged that "Mrs. Mary" had the white tower at La Finca built in 1947.

I remarked that I was given to understand it was in the White Tower where Papa did his writing. Hemingway turned towards me and grinning stated, "That's bullshit! The first floor of the tower is the cat's home! There's a bathroom on the second floor, and on the top floor is a work place -- which I don't use -- and a library of military books."

"Then where do you do your writing?" I asked.

"In my bedroom standing up." Hemingway informed nonchalantly.

Strolling about the fence-enclosed 15 acres of La Finca I became intoxicated with the array of tropical botanical delights: Over a dozen different kinds of mangoes grew on the long slope from the main gate up to the house; a variety of flowers, tall royal palms, areca palms, coral trees, ferns, and clumps of sweet smelling lippa. In addition, there was a generous vegetable garden that contained beans, tomatoes, egg plant, etc. and numerous fruit trees containing limes, great fruit, coconuts, oranges, papaya, bananas, etc. Further, there was a cow pasture with a half-dozen cows.

Circumnavigating the property, we came full circle and Papa with a content smile commented, "My fortress from the world Shadow! Ya know, this was once a white limestone villa. Hell, the only thing white now is the tower. She may be crumbling a little, but she's got dignity -- my charming shack!" Papa laughed. "Ya know this place has a wine cellar?" Hemingway asked.

"No; I didn't know that," I replied, "but I do now."

Again, Hemingway laughed. Walking up the steps of the terrace Hemingway and I made our way to the swimming pool area where Papa motioned me to take a chair. I seated myself comfortably in an old wooden chair, put my legs and feet straight out in front of me, and admired the large rectangular swimming pool with its crystal clear deliciously enticing water. A gentle, cool, caressing northeast breeze was gliding over the swimming pool water generating a shimmer that produced hundreds of glimmering tiny lights. In the background were white trellises with magnificent bougainvillea securely clinging to the wooden structures. I felt totally relaxed, tired, elated -- somewhere between the fields of ambrosia and the seventh plateau of joy -- when my "willing suspension of disbelief' was shattered by Papa's high pitched voice asking, "Shadow, ya wanna night cap?"

"Ya, sure, why not?" I replied.

"Wadda ya want?" Papa inquired.

Smiling, I responded with, "How about an "E. Hemingway Special?"

Sitting next to me in another wooden chair, Hemingway leaned forward, started laughing and commented, "Ah, shit, you've been to El Floridita and met Jesus!"

"That I have," I confirmed. "Jesus Christ that Jesus can talk. I swear he's got diarrhea of the mouth! But just when you're about to get pissed off at him for his perpetual yapping, he'll flash you one of his big angelic smiles and then it's hard to get irritated with the guy! I'll tell ya 'Mrs. Mary' loves him. But, hell, he's a great bar man-- and don't mess around with the guy 'cause he'll probably kick the shit out of ya. He's taken boxing lessons," Hemingway concluded.

"He's got what the Irish call a lot of 'blarney,' or the 'gift of the gab," I remarked.

"He's got what I call a steady stream of floral bullshit!" Hemingway countered. We both leaned back in our chairs and laughed. "But like I said," Papa reiterated, "he's a hell of a barman."

"That he is," I concurred "Everyone at El Floridita likes him so I'm sure he'll stay there."

"Oh, hell, yes," Papa confirmed, "He's got security there."

Rene came over to Hemingway and I from the house and handed me my "E. Hemingway Special" in what looked like something between a large bowel and a small bucket. He handed Hemingway a large tumbler with an amber liquid.

"Scotch," Papa smiled, "with water. It's neater at night."

"Earlier, Papa, when we were having lunch you commented that immigrants were the easy prey politically for politicians when anti-immigration sentiment was high and that odious actions were justified by invoking the claim that such action was taken in the name of "National Security" when voices of concern were raised. Exactly what did you mean?" I queried.

Hemingway sat motionless for a few seconds staring at the swimming pool, took a gulp of Scotch, drew a deep breath, and stated, "Shadow, I've seen innocent, terrified people subjected to horror and have privation heaped upon them all in the name of 'National Security.' After, World War I when I was a correspondent living in Paris I covered the conflict between Turkey and Greece and I saw the carnage the Turks exacted upon the Greeks -- much of it, they claimed, in the name of 'National Security.' When I was in Spain I witnessed the butchery and slaughter that members and supporters of the Nationalists inflicted upon supporters of the Loyalists. Men, woman, children, the old, young, members of non-political groups were all fair game for the Nationalists. Jesus Christ, a translator for a friend of mine who had no political affiliations what so ever was pulled out of a bar by National Police and shot because a suspected Loyalists simply said "Hello" to him! (Hemingway was referring to Professor Robles who was a translator for Hemingway's friend, the writer John Dos Passos). Oh, hell, I'm not saying the Loyalists were all clean; they committed their share of executions, but they were more honest -- theirs was for revenge -- not for a claim of 'National Security."

Before Hemingway could continue I asked in a tongue-in-cheek fashion, "What the hell exactly is 'National Security'?"

Hemingway looked at me and calmly stated, "It's a policy that governments use to silence critics and the opposition. Therefore, it's whatever a government wants it to be. In the Soviet Union the government uses it as an instrument to repress anyone or any group who they maintain could represent a threat to the State -- especially anyone or any group with new ideas. In Nazi Germany it was a tool utilized by the government to silence those who opposed or questioned the wishes of the State. In many of the Latin American and Caribbean Countries it's an apparatus to crush any challenge to the ruling "junta" by those calling for change. Remember, Shadow, one of the things most feared in Latin American Countries is change and the developing of a middle class which brings change."

I took a sip of my drink from the 'bucket' and followed up with, "So there exists a common denominator applicable to all states regardless if politically those states are to the right or left."

"Absolutely!" Papa confirmed. "When it comes to human rights, you know the only difference between the Communist and the Fascist?"

I confessed to not being certain.

"Let me put it to you basically, Shadow," Hemingway stated leaning forward in his chair, "if the goddamn Fascists think you're a threat to the state and spot you walking down the street, they will grab ya by the ass and blow your brains out right there. In contrast, if the goddamn Communists think you're a threat to the state and spot you walking down the street, they will grab ya by the shoulder, escort ya down an ally, and then blow your brains out. The end result with both forms of governments varies in degree but not in kind. Shit, this is basically what I said back in 1937 at The America writer's Congress in New York City!

"So, I responded, "'National Security' is far more than a government policy-- it's a philosophy."

"No, Hemingway quickly replied, "'National Security' is an ideology. In all cases with any nation -- including the United States -- there is a common pattern, a common network of repression, a common strategy and, behind it all, a common ideology -- the ideology of 'National Security." Papa continued with, "The 'National Security' ideology is not a matter of simple brutality and pathological behavior. Shit all, it's a matter of war! I get black ass when I think of Argentina and their military who express it as, Our struggle for 'National Security' doesn't know moral or natural limits, it is beyond good and evil. I'm gonna tell ya something Shadow, so listen up well! The essential concepts of the 'National Security' ideology are: the individual person does not exist, people are myths. What really exist are nations. But the nation is interchangeable with the state. Without the state, the nation is nothing. And the state is embodied in the government.

"The state is an organ which has to defend itself, to strengthen itself and to be combative. Expanding nations, looking for vital space and economic opportunities, have to be in a state of permanent war: war against the individual adversary, war against outside powers or ideologies, war against communism! The war is total: it mobilizes all citizens, civil and military; all people and countries are involved. All human activities are acts of war. The enemy has infiltrated everywhere."

"Shit all, I remember the God damn military in Argentina saying, "If obliged to, in Argentina, all the necessary persons will die in order to achieve the security of the nation."

"Shadow, National Security' doesn't ask about means, violent or nonviolent. National Security' is absolute. National Security" makes no distinction between internal or external policy: the enemy is inside or outside the country. There is no difference between the army or the police, for they face the same problem, they fight the same enemy. The police exist not to protect citizens but to protect 'the system."

Feeling something between anxious and alarmed with what Hemingway was relating I took a large swallow of my daiquiri, leaned back in my chair, put my fist to my head, and inquired, "I can understand how Fascist nations, the 'Reds,' and Latin American "junta" come to embrace the ideology of 'National Security,' but you said the United States has not been immune from the National Security paranoia. From where and when did we get this ideology?"

Oh, shit!" Hemingway said. "It's not so new. It was Nazi ideology of the state, and it was in Germany that the science of 'geo-politics' was born. Later the French followed the doctrine in their colonial war against Algeria. And it's the doctrine adopted by the United States after the Second World War to justify participation in wars outside the United States, as a means of protecting 'National Security' at large. Fuck all! Hemingway declared. "Look what happened about five years ago in Guatemala. The poor country was on the balls of their ass economically! The people lived like garbage dump dogs; so a few brave souls pushed for economic, educational, and health reforms for workers and the people. Tragically, while they were pressing their reform issues with the government of Guatemala they failed to take into consideration that the actual 'dark' government of Guatemala was not the Guatemalan officials but UNITED FRUIT! These United son-of-a-bitches controlled over half the usable land in Guatemala and owned almost all the railroads. Almost 40,000 Guatemalans slaved for United Fruit and were paid 50 cents a day!"

"When was this?" I asked.

I believe this was 1952," Papa said. "Anyway", Hemingway continued, "so when these United Fruit bastards get wind of the reform issues being pressed by these few courageous "descamisados" they immediately run to the Department. of State and started screaming that they were 'communist' taking over the government of Guatemala. John Foster Dulles -- ya know dull duller Dulles -- who is Secretary of State immediately refers the matter to the CIA, that is being run by his dumb ass brother, Allen Dulles, who sends in a bunch of heavily armed psychopathic assassins supported by some air cover to butcher and slaughter some dirt poor farmers only because they wanted for their kids a little piece of a better life. Then, after the return of the CIA's 'black angel' the Department of State swaggered about Washington belching platitudes about how our government saved a South American Nations from the 'communist boogeyman.'"

"All in the name of 'National Security?" I commented.

"All in the name of 'National Security.' In this case 'National Security' translated to United Fruit's economic imperialism." Papa confirmed.

Turning in his chair sideways and looking at me Hemingway offered, "I'm gonna give ya a little advise Shadow. When ya start to gain some success with ya writing, ya better be careful of what ya write."

Okay, I thought, and then inquired with, "Have you ever had any representatives from any of our government agencies -- known or unknown -- bother you?"

Hemingway flashed a big smile and acknowledged, "Shit, all, Shadow, I've got the FBI on my ass!"

Surprised, I blurted out with, "Jesus Christ, for what?"

With an expression that was a half smile and half contempt Papa explained as to how he believed it started in 1937 with his first trip to Spain when he took part in the filming of the documentary THE SPANISH EARTH. Then, on his return to the United States, he made his first political speech -- at Carnegie Hall in June, 1937 before League of American Authors Congress (The America Writer's

Congress) against Fascism and next went to Hollywood to private functions to raise funds for the purchase of ambulances for the Spanish Republic. Next, with August '42 and the United States now Britain's ally in the Second World War, how he created the now famous Crook Factory, a private undertaking whose self-appointed mission was to investigate the pro-Nazi factions in Cuba. Its headquarters were La Finca Vigia and until 1943 its undercover agents -- fisherman, priests, waiters, pimps, and whores -- collected information on the Spanish Falangists on the island. Later, he reached a decision and decided to disband so at to concentrate all efforts on sub-hunting with the PILAR with the idea to harass any German submarines that might be lurking in the Gulf of Mexico. When I asked why the FBI would harass him for what appeared to be clearly patriotic activities, Hemingway related it was because he had accused the Department of State of failing to respond to warnings about Fascist activities in Cuba and South West Mexico where there existed strong Fascist sentiments.

To this disclosure I remarked, "Nazis in Mexico; you were in Mexico? I never read or heard anything about you being in Mexico!"

Hemingway shot me a glance and asked philosophically, "When do you ever really know someone?", and followed up with, "Hell yes I was in Mexico, in 1942. I obtained a lot of significant information and data on German activities there and gave the stuff to our Department of State who proceeded to go and chase butterflies or turn up the volume on Wagner. Shit, I still have a lot of that information inside in an old box".

"What kind of information?" I asked.

"Shit, I gave our Department of State a full description of a German pharmaceutical company called I. G. Farben, which served as a cover for agents of the Third Reich. I also gave a report on the relationship between the German ambassador to Mexico and a group of right-wing intellectuals. One of these, a doctor, received money from the Germans to publish anti-Semitic literature. In addition, the same document contained a study of Nazi activities in the coffee-growing area of Chiapas de Sononusco, where most of the haciendas were owned by Germans, obvious recruits for the Third Reich party. I described the zone as very remote and therefore of strategic importance." looked over at Hemingway with an expression of resolve and commented, "Shades of the famous Zimmermann Letter.

While observing some birds frolicking about the swimming pool, Papa offered, "Oh, hell we Americans have always suffered from historical amnesia."

Massaging Hemingway's commentary concerning his being stalked by the FBI, I allowed as to how this could be attributed to a writer's over-active imagination fueled by a lifetime of exposure and participation in the major events of the theaters of the world. Nevertheless, it would not be until many years later -- long after Hemingway's death -- with the passage of the Federal Freedom of Information Act that the world learned that, indeed, the FBI had been spying on Hemingway and that Papa's apprehensions were justified.

As Hemingway spoke, his mood transformed from one of heretofore light humor, to intensity, to darkness. Evidence of this was demonstrated in the force with which he spoke, the inflection placed on specific words, and at times, his body language. Here was a man who was driven by belief, shaped by conviction and who had witnessed and experienced courage, carnage, betrayal, loyalty, and had written tersely and succinctly about these attributes. Now, as I sat and listened to Papa's commentary his statements moved from the position of anger to that of bitterness over what he perceived to be betrayal by governments to the many who had fallen over the years in the service of their countries.

In the years following his death Hemingway's statements relevant to "National Security," especially for we who lived in America, were to be chillingly prophetic as we viewed a panorama of our governments agencies with it's painful and tragic involvement in Vietnam, the botched and blunders of our CIA and their ALPHA 66 members who invaded Cuba, the absurdity and imbecility of the FBI with their attempts at besmirching the honor of Dr. Martin Luther King, the breaking into the offices of psychiatrist, the National Guard and their murdering of students at Kent State, the beating and bludgeoning of reporters, students, and citizens by the Chicago Police, the CIA and National Security Council and their policies of genocide against Indians and farmers in Nicaragua and Guatemala, the blunders and lies of Bosnia and Somalia and so on and so forth. All of this, according to the people who stood -- and stand -- in the shadows of our government and did so in the name of "National Security" and as they spoke of God and democracy on their lips did so with the blood of the innocent on their hands. Stretching his arms above his head Hemingway let go with a big yawn and commented that he missed his afternoon "siesta", and then looking over in my direction asked if I wanted a "night cap". Assuring Papa I had enough to drink Hemingway asked if 1 wanted to take a swim in the pool before retiring to the guest house. I informed Papa I did not bring a bathing suit whereupon Hemingway quipped, "Shit! Go in bare ass -- Ava Gardner always does!"

"The actress, Ava Gardner?" I inquired.

"Hell yes! She's a good egg! Likes to swim bare ass, drinks like a fish, has a foul mouth and cusses like a drunken sailor, but is a hell of a good egg," Papa verified.

Again, I declined the invitation to skinny dip whereupon Hemingway asked me if I wanted to take a battery-powered portable Zenith radio to the guest house. I also declined this offer, but asked if I could borrow one of the books from the library, to which Papa asked,

"Which one?"

In an attempt to be ingratiating I responded, "Maybe one of your volumes of short stories."

Hemingway titled his head to the right and replied, "Oh, shit!". Then, rising out of his chair Hemingway beckoned me to follow him inside to the living room with shelves of books. Walking over to the east-side of the room Papa retrieved a volume from the shelf and asked, "Do ya know Markham?" I confessed I did not. To this reply Hemingway handed me a volume which was entitled WEST WITH THE NIGHT by Beryl Markham. As I examined the volume Papa continued with, "The broads a cheap thief, a social parasite, likes to kick back with the booze, and can be a real bitch, but God damn she can write!"

Innocently I asked, "Do you know her? Is she still alive?"

"Ya," Papa said, "I know her. I met her on my first trip to Africa where she spent most of her life, in what was East Africa and now Kenya. I think she lives near Nairobi. She's had a number of fucked up relations with men, but the more ya read of her work's Shadow, ya can forget about some bullshit ya see in print about one of her husbands, a Raoul Schumacher, a Hollywood hack who some claim actually wrote this book. As I said, this is bullshit. The broad can write!"

Hemingway turned from me and called for Rene to escort me to the guest house as it was now dark. While awaiting Rene's arrival I asked what time I was to join Papa for breakfast to which he responded I was simply, upon rising, to come up to La Finca and Lety or Rene would provide me with breakfast. As for himself, he and Juan were leaving early to attend to some business in Cojimar, about five miles east of Havana and would return to La Finca in the late morning or around noon time. I thanked Papa for everything, which he quickly dismissed, and bid him good night.

As Rene and I began walking to the guest house I observed light one each side of La Finca's property and inquired of Rene what they were. I was informed that they were neighbors, one was a Pedro Buscaron who Papa liked and respected and the other was a Frank Steinhart, Jr. who Papa detested. With the moving closer to the guest cottage and farther away from La Finca, I noticed that the lights of La Finca were on and asked Rene if this was standard. Rene assured me it was and that this became common practice, a left over from some years past when it seemed every day and evening was a "fiesta."

Sometimes Hollywood film stars lounged by the swimming pool, drinking whisky; flamenco dancers and toreros sipped vintage Cuban rum to the sound of music. Rene said this was the gay, easy going aspect of La Finca where events always ended in laughter. It was an all the year party and dazzling, so glamorous, so literary that the manner in which Rene described the setting it was something out of a B movie. Still, as Rene related the movie sometimes was more like a slapstick comedy. Like the time Hemingway lay in wait for his one next door neighbor/enemy Frank Steinhart and then hurled stink bombs and firecrackers into his garden just as he was giving a grand reception. There were also the Sundays spent in illegal betting on baseball championship games, something Hemingway tolerated, even though he was manager of the local San Francisco de Paula team, Las Estrellas.

Rene continued on with how on other days Hemingway would place bets on his fighting cocks. At one time he had as many as twenty birds at La Finca; and they were looked after by the gardener, Jose Herrero, whose nickname was Pilicho. A magnificent, white tailed champion once earned Papa $800.00. In later years I would learn that when Hemingway made his will, he left his cocks to Pilicho, just as he gave his beloved PILAR to Gregorio Fuentes, some of his rifles including his .22 caliber Winchester to Rene and the meadow adjoining La Finca Vigia to his neighbor Pedro Buscaron, who had always been particularly helpful.

Approximately 100 feet to the front of the guesthouse I was startled to hear the night air suddenly filled with bagpipes playing AULD LANG SYNE! Inquiring of Rene as to the source of the music he related that Hemingway was playing records on the phonograph which he sometimes did as a way of "winding down" for the day. Arriving at the guesthouse, Rene unlocked the door and put on the lights. Entering behind Rene I observed the interior of the guest cottage and found it to be Spartan, but adequate to the occasion. I thanked Rene for his accompaniment and conversation to which he responded with a sheepish grin and the comment, "No hay de que." as he left to return to main house and his duties. Unpacking my meager belongings from the overnight bag I stored them away followed by my removing Papa's guayabera that Juan had given to me earlier in the morning and placed it on a wooden hanger. Next, I undressed and laid out flat on the bed and stared at the ceiling for a few moments after which I took the book WEST WITH THE NIGHT that Hemingway had given to me and began moving through the pages; and , as Papa had said Markam's words were captivating and engrossing. Unfortunately, as I lie upon the bed, my body tired and my mind weary I was finding it difficult to concentrate on the contents of the text. Moreover, I began to reflect upon the fact that the bed upon which I was laying was the same that heretofore personalities and celebrities such as Marlene Dietrich, Malcolm Cowley, Ava Gardner, Arnold Gingrich, etc. prostrated themselves upon. With this realization dancing about in my mind I closed the book and placed it next to me while at the same time I closed my heavy eyes and evoked the reality that my visit with Hemingway and my stay at La Finca Vigia was a journey to a Tropical Camelot with Papa as it's Arthur. My "willing suspension of disbelief' had catapulted me into a historical Garden Of Eden wherein Hemingway held forth for almost twenty years the necessary, self imposed ascent towards "ngaje ngai," the House Of God belief and ritual in the pursuit of immortality. Still, I had met Hemingway; the man who could make everyday a fiesta but who I observed preferred cool evenings with his cats, dogs, and a cool drink, a very simple man, a man quite different from the legendary Papa and the never-ending tales of heroic events and sensational activities, a man who could enjoy the times when there were no foreign visitors to disrupt the normal rhythms of life in La Finca Vigia. I could envision Hemingway in the evenings reading a book, a magazine such as the NEW YORKER, or else THE NEW YORK TIMES. I could see him finishing off any leftover wine from dinner and soon grow sleepy and say "buenas noches" to all, takes his leave before midnight. In the morning, after several hours of writing, and perhaps an "eye opener," I could see Hemingway's blissful peace being shattered by the arrival of Rene with the mail: letters and postcards from friends, bills, never ending business with publishers and film producers, and all the nuisance letters you get when you are successful and famous. In addition there was always Papa's running battle with one reviewer or another; many of them seemed to relish tearing his work to pieces. With these snapshots dancing about him my mind forming a wonderful picturesque kaleidoscope of an Eden past and present I felt my exhausted and spent brain drained and collectively melt into the configuration of the beds mattress.

It had been a long day.

Illustrations:

The large living room of La Finca Vigia reflected the personality of the man who had utilized it for almost a quarter of a century – large, unique, strong, and charming.

Close up: Note that it was in this room that the author after drying off from a tropical downpour, and being provided a 'body warmer" by Papa, (a full glass of Old Grand Dad Bourbon

Whisky) from the table between the chairs and that the author and Hemingway embarked upon one of many fascinating conversations over a matter of days.

The large living room of La Finca Vigia, with books everywhere.

The sheer volume of Papa's library was shocking at first. And to receive a gift from this library was an unexpected surprise.

The author was given this card to the Biltmore Kennel Club in Playa de Marianao with instructions to present it to the manager, Vincente Monterey with comments that the card was from "Mr. Way" whereupon the author was assured of Gaining admittance to a splendid private club along with a free drink. The author never attempted to redeem the offer.

Chapter 3
Botanas, Cojimar, Key West, HUAC, Dinner,
Latin American Foreign Policy, and All That

My deep slumber was shattered by a symphony consisting of crowing roosters, barking dogs, mooing cows, meowing cats, and chirping birds. With nature's introduction to the morning, I glanced at my Timex watch -- "it keeps on ticking after a licking" and noted it was 7:59 a.m. As I rose from the bed from whence I had spent the night somewhere between the lingering spirits of Marlene Dietrich and Ava Gardner, I felt and smelled a sweet cool tropical breeze which was accompanied by shafts of bright orange and yellow light which had entered through the window and pierced my eyes. It was going to be another one of those legendary "lousy days in the Caribbean" I thought.

Completing the ritual of morning clean up I dressed, tucked my overnight bag in a corner, and straightened up the bed covers a best as I could, turned off the fan and the lamp light that was on the table next to the bed, and walked out of the guest house closing the door securely behind me. Then, as I slowly walked up the slope towards La Finca with WEST WITH THE NIGHT secured under my arm I felt a slight twinge in my stomach reminding me that I was missing my coffee and bread. As the front door being the only entrance of La Finca with which I was familiar I circled around to that point, once again climbed the stairs to the terrace, once again cautiously stepping around the piles of animal droppings -- some fresh -- and once again knocked loudly on the front door, and once again it swung open with a perplexed Lety -- void of her usually contagious smile -- staring at me and presented the question, "Por que usted no uso el otro la puerta?"

To which I replied diplomatically that I did not know the other entrances to La Finca. Lety managed a sheepish smile, told me to enter. She pointed to the things on the table and asked if I would like desayuno. I assured her I did and was subsequently directed to the dining room where I took the same chair I had used at lunch the day before. Shortly, Rene entered with a large tray that contained coffee, a bowl of raw sugar, and cream, Cuban bread, a bowl of raw honey, butter, papaya, mangos, citrus marmalade, and orange juice. I feasted after which I informed Rene I was going out by the pool area whereupon I selected the same chair I had sat in the night before, opened WEST WITH THE NIGHT and read relaxed. Upon finishing Beryl Markham's work I entered La Finca and proceeded to the living room and returned the book to the exact location from - whence Hemingway had taken it the previous evening. As I was leaving the large living room with all its opulence I spotted Lety -- now wearing her captivating expression and related to her I was going to take a walk around La Finca. Descending the steps of the terrace I undertook a slow relaxing stroll among the trees, colorful foliage, and grass. I was unsure how long I had been roaming about La Finca for time had melted during my leisurely wanderings. Then, my tranquility was interrupted when I heard a high pitched voice call out, "How ya doing there, Shadow? Did ya get some grub?"

"Yes, Lety and the kitchen put out a great spread," I intoned. "Did you get your business taken care of in Havana?" I probed.

"Hell, I didn't have any business and I didn't go to Havana. I went to Cojimar to check on some fuel lines for the PILAR," Hemingway stated.

"Oh," I remarked, "I would have liked to have gone with you. I like boats."

Hemingway sported one of those wide impish smiles of his and challenged, "You told me ya like bay and flat fishing; ya never mentioned ya like boats. Besides, I figured ya would have wanted to sleep in. Anyway, Juan and I were out of here by 7:30 a.m.

"I was up at 7:59 a.m.," I verified. "I always get up early and greet the morning."

"Me to," Hemingway acknowledged, "I get most of my important work done before noon, regardless of what it is." Still sporting his wide impish grin Papa proposed, "Let's get something to eat and drink." He looked at me and concluded with, "Don't be down about the PILAR, you'll get to see her another time."

Although it had been awhile since I had breakfast, the idea of a new adventure out of the kitchen of La Finca was an exciting prospect -- and the notion of a drink held great promise. I walked through the front door of La Finca, again, with Hemingway a few steps ahead of me. He marched directly towards the dining room still flashing a big grin and bellowing "Que tal?" to all within the household he saw. Next, Papa moved to one side of the dining room table to take his usual seat, and I following in like manner moved to the other side of the table to what was rapidly becoming my "usual" seat directly across from Hemingway and assumed a comfortable position. Within a few moments the shy, yet confident Lety entered and forthwith Papa issued instructions to bring "botanas" and followed up with "Wadda ya want to drink, Shadow? We got some cold beer."

"Ya got some more of the red table wine that we had yesterday? I'll have some of that if ya do," I replied.

"Shit!" Papa expressed. "We got oceans of that stuff"

"Papa," I stated, "you said you went to Cojimar this morning and every time I hear that and close my eyes I can see Spencer Tracy portraying Santiago in his skiff cutting up the Bonita to eat."

Hemingway smiled and commented, "Ya got a good image of him because he was sober, for the most part, at least on screen."

I acknowledged Papa's statement with, "I read where he likes to drink."

"Likes to drink? Tracy's a goddamn lush! Christ, he didn't even arrive in Havana to start shooting the film on time. Christ, Katie Hepburn had to come down to Miami and drag his drunken ass out of a Miami Beach Hotel where he was on a bender and put him on a flight to Havana!" Hemingway announced.

"I saw Tracy in CAPTAINS COURAGEOUS when he played the role of Manuel, the Portuguese pescadoro. I thought he did a good job," I offered. Before Hemingway could respond to my assessment of Tracy's performance I asked, "Tell me Papa, how close did Tracy come to your Santiago?"

"Not very close," Hemingway confirmed. "Tracy's size wasn't right."

"How come he got the role of Santiago?" I continued "I'm sure you had some input as to who would make an effective Santiago."

"Tracy had some rights to the film and there wasn't much I could do about that,"

Hemingway explained.

Next, I ventured a question that had always vexed me, "Papa, who is Santiago?"

Hemingway pressed his lips together hard, leaned back in his chair, looked directly at me and revealed, "Santiago is Gregorio Fuentes, he's Anselmo Hernandez, he's all of the Cuban Pescadoros -- he's me! Santiago is someone I have thought about for many years."

"I've always admired and respected the pescadoros and their small crafts which they venture out into the Gulf. " I acknowledged.

"Shadow, these Cuban pescadoros -- like the pescadoros from the Yucatan Peninsula of Mexico -- are hewed from stern stuff. They are like the skiffs they take into the unforgiving sea -- strong, steady, reliable, and unpretentious. They are a consequence of the time their land reflects and the faith to which they were born. They are capable of enduring the unendurable and of suffering the insufferable." As Hemingway spoke, his mood changed from one of lightheartedness to one of somberness.

Years later I owned a food processing business in Puerto Progreso, in the Yucatan, of Mexico. I routinely dealt and traded with the Cuban fisherman who would put in at Puerto Progreso to trade their catch for items they could not buy in Fidel's so called "Workers paradise." I developed a more acute appreciation and understanding of the material from which these fishermen were; as Papa had said, 'hewed.' My appreciation included members of my own family. These colorful men, who put out to sea in their colorful crafts before the sun rose assured of nothing but hard work, scorching sun or wrathful waters, long hours, dangers and loneliness. All of this to put a pot of rice and beans with some tortillas or bread on the table, and maybe if they were lucky that day some chicken. If the heavens smiled on them and they had a good catch, got back to the quay before the price for fish began to fall, than with the little extra money they may receive for their toil they could pay off the medical bills they incurred when their children were ill, and their children were always ill, or buy them some new sandals. Just as Hemingway was about to speak he dropped his napkin on the floor and bent down for it. With its retrieval, and before he could comment, I stated, "I've read, and have been given to understand by some reviewers that THE OLD MAN AND THE SEA was metaphorical and, indeed, contained almost mystical qualities."

In response to my statement, Hemingway's face and mood transformed from that of previous somberness to humor. Leaning forward and putting his both big forearms on the table Papa clasp his hands and replied, "I heard all that horseshit before; that's Michener, (James A. Michener). Hell, he's a good egg, a right kind of guy. But I'm gonna whisper something in your ear about writing, Shadow. People don't see in literature what is there -- they see only what they want to see. In that regard they are like cheap ass politicians! Now, let me line it up straight so ya get it right. THE OLD MAN AND THE SEA like I told ya is a story I thought about for years -- and it's a goddamn good story. It's a story about an old fisherman who simply went out in the Gulf too far! That's it -- nothing more!"

With this information tucked away in the back of my mind, I was tempted to ask Hemingway if any parallel could be drawn between the young lions that Santiago recalled and the leopard that lost its way up on Mt. Kilimanjaro. Wisdom coached me not to. Through the dining room door area Lety came into the room with a "garrafa de vino tinto" and a glass; both items she put in front of me. In front of Hemingway she put a large frosted glass that Hemingway described as "one hell of a Tom Collins."

Following the drinks, Lety brought in several large platters containing plates with food and bowls of soup in addition to Cuban bread, tortillas, and soda crackers. With the plates and bowls upon the table and drinks in hand, Papa held court and proceeded to explain that the spread represented a Cuban/Mexican setting and began identifying each dish. Initially, was the soup, "sopa de lime", (line soup), consisting of a delicious chicken stock with shredded chicken, lime juice, black pepper, tortillas. Next, there was "papadzules", chopped hard boiled eggs rolled up in tortillas and covered with a smooth pumpkin seed sauce. This was followed by "panuchos", a handmade tortilla but cut open and filled with refried beans. Finally, there was "ceviches", raw fish mixed with diced tomatoes, onions, cylantro, lime juice, black pepper and salt. With the completion of the explanation, Papa ordered, "Dig in!"

As we ate and drank we discussed an array of topics that ranged from: smoking fish and meat, making beer, clam chowder, omelets, meat loaf, rowing boats, old movies, dogs, cats, birds, gold fish, turtles, mice, beaches, trees, vegetables, and plants. Commenting on the outstanding taste of the "botanas," I remarked as to how I could understand the kitchen of La Finca coming by their great Cuban recipes, but how did the kitchen acquire the Mexican recipes?

Hemingway replied that when he was in Mexico he had visited a number of locals in the State of Yucatan; specifically, the Capital, Merida, Uxmal, Rio Lagartos, Telchac, Muna, and a few other places he did not recall the names of.

As I finished my "sopa de lime" I inquired of Hemingway if he had made any return trips via the PILAR or other modes of transportation to Key West. Hemingway, developing something between disappointment and displeasure on his brow stated unequivocally, "NO." I offered that in past years I had visited the keys and Key West with my father, uncle, and grandfather to do some bone fishing and that I had found they are unique with its foliage, waters, history, individual keys connected with several dozen bridges, an concluding with Key West, itself, but some 80 plus miles from Havana. With my overview, Hemingway assumed a more tranquil posture and related as to how he used to love the Keys, "before they got fucked up!"

Before I could ask Hemingway to clarify, he continued on relating that a "one eyed Portuguese bastard" friend of his (the writer John Dos Passos) had initially told him about the Keys. I took a large swallow of the "delightful red table wine" and, somewhat solicitously offered that "The Keys must have been a paradise when you first went there Papa." Hemingway now leaned forward, again placed his big forearms on the dining room table, and again clasped his hands. This was a characteristic of Hemingway's I quickly learned that signaled Papa was about to hold court on a particular topic; and, on the topic of Key West he did not disappoint me.

"Yea", Hemingway started, then pausing. "When I first got there from Europe in '28 for me at first it was pure hell with the heat and humidity. My second wife and I (Papa's second wife was Pauline Pfeiffer) stayed at a place called Casa Antigua. Christ it was hot! We made several trips to Key West after the initial one. There was something primitive, yet; honest, sincere, secluded, and exciting about the Keys at that time that attracted me to the place. So, in a couple of years we bought a place there. Shit, it was an old run down place one a piece of land that was over an acre -- a lot of land in the Keys -- built in the l 850's by a guy in the shipping business. "That's the house on Whitehead Street," I injected.

"Ya, that's the one; Ya been in it?" Hemingway asked.

"No," I replied, "but I've passed it several times."

"Well my wife fixed the place up the way she wanted it -- European style – not necessarily my taste; but it gave me the peace and tranquility I needed to work. Also, the exterior activities for relaxation were terrific! Hell, like I told ya yesterday, it was in Key

West that I learned and took up the sport of bill fishing! And when I'd get back from a trip out with the PILAR I could "wet my whistle" at the local "spirits emporium."

"That would be Sloppy Joes," I again injected.

"Ya," Hemingway confirmed, "but the joint was known first as The Blind Pig. When old Josie got the joint he named it Sloppy Joe's. The name fit him. Later, old Josie moved Sloppy Joe's a block north to the corner of Green and Duval. I think old Josie got all pissed off over a buck increase in the rent. But, hell, it was a great watering hole! All of the local fisherman came there along with an assortment of "Conchs", drifters, boozers, bull-shiters, and other wonderful, swell guys. Old Josie, he kept the joint for a long time; until he died, right here in Cuba." Papa was referring to Joe Russell, an adventurer and longtime Hemingway pal. Papa used Josie as a model for one of his characters.

As Hemingway spoke recalling his early days in Key West he smiled fondly while Rene or Lety would periodically enter the dining room to check on my supply or red table wine and to freshen Papa's large glass of Tom Collins.

"Who made up most of the population of Key West at the turn of the century?" I asked.

Taking a large gulp from a fresh Tom Collins, Hemingway squinted his eyes and related, "Well ya had the Negro's who mostly lived in 'Bahama Town' and who worked mainly in the seafood businesses or in the standard businesses like restaurants, stores, and such. Then ya had native 'Conchs,' born in the Keys, mostly from Florida 'cracker' families who came earlier from parts of Florida north of the Keys, but not always. Ya had some Conchs whose families came from Europe in the last century (eighteenth century), like good old Charlie Thompson, a swell guy, who came to Key West and did very well. Hell, the Thompson Family owned a lot of operations like The Turtle Kraals, Thompson's Docks, a fleet of fishing boats, a seafood processing company, a fleet of trucks, an icehouse, a marine hardware and tackle shop, and a shit pot full of other operations. Yet Charlie Thompson like old Josie was an okay guy, a good egg even though the family had bucks. Swell people. Then there were the Cubans who had been in Key West for generations. They were in the cigar business -- and cigars were big business in Key West -- just like in your Tampa Bay area."

76

"My grandfather, who had visited Key West before my father, uncle and I, mentioned there was a well to do guy who made money in the marine salvage business," I remarked.

"Salvage business my ass!" Hemingway guffawed. "That was Captain John Geiger! That nutty old bastard was nothing but a pirate, a thief, and a crook! Oh, shit, he made a bucket of bucks and build a great big house for the Geiger family -- but he was nothing but a goddamn pirate!"

I continued with, "Also, Papa, my grandfather said that when he was in Key West he heard form a local bartender about a strange demented doctor who was involved with necrophilia. Is there anything to that story?"

Hemingway developed a somber expression and related, "Ya, that was a fucked up guy who called himself Count Dr. Karl Von Kessel. He practiced medicine in Key West and claimed to have six medical degrees from German Universities. Hell, who knows? Anyway, at that time in the cigar factories where the Cubans worked tuberculosis was a scourge among the workers. In point of fact, it was a scourge in Key West for many years; but, it hit the Cubans particularly hard what with working in close quarters, hot, humid, lots of tobacco dust, and long hours. Well, in one of the cigar factories there was a young, beautiful, vivacious woman named Elena Hoyos. At the various fiestas she was always the darling, sought after, and everyone man's dream. Tragically, she developed tuberculosis and sought help from the medical community within Key West. Unfortunately, at that time, there wasn't anything the physicians could do except prolong the obvious consequences of the ravaging disease. So, in desperation, this poor gorgeous gal goes to Count Dr. Karl Von Kessel seeking some sort of magical cure. Also, the doctor claims to be a sculpture that works in wax and wants to use Elena Hoyos as a model so there is no fee charged by the Count Doctor for the gal's office visits. Well, hell. There was no cure for tuberculosis so the young gal got worse and died. But the Count Doctor during the gal's terrible illness falls deeply in love with his beautiful patient and after her death ask the gal's family if he could have built for her a burial chamber as a proper place for her to rest, and because the Count Doctor understands the families economic condition states that he will do the embalming of the gal free. The family agrees, and this old fart who is more than twice the gal's age visits the burial chamber every night. Then, one night after about six months the crazy old bastard steals Elena's body from the burial chamber and brings it to his home! Now, with Elena's body undergoing decay this old lunatic removes all her burial clothing and dresses her in a magnificent gown and proceeds to reconstruct her decaying, once beautiful face, out of wax!"

"Jesus Christ, that's like something right out of THE HOUSE OF WAX with Vincent Price!" I impulsively uttered.

"Right," Hemingway acknowledged and continued with, "Well, now it get even more bizarre because the "Old Count Doctor" keeps Elena's corpse in his house for over six years! However, Elena's sister becomes suspicious because the doctor never lets anyone in the burial chamber and he has the only key. Finally, after continued rebuffs by Count Doctor, Elena's sister goes to the local authorities who enter the deranged Count Doctor's house make the macabre discovery and arrest the demented old bastard. There's a hearing, but no trial. Everyone in Key West knew what happened, but the officials wanted to down play the whole thing so that the Keys didn't get the reputation of being home to an unhinged old fart. Well, Elena was finally put to rest in a spot known only to a few people. The depth of the Count Doctor's madness was disclosed by the coroner's office after they examined what was left of Elena's remains and it was discovered that this sick lunatic had been fucking Elena's corpse for all those years!"

"Jesus Christ!" I noisily uttered.

"How do ya like them apples?" Hemingway stated and finished with "The final chapter occurred shortly after the informal hearing involving the Count Doctor and with the Count Doctor's release from jail based on the fact that no official charges were filed against him. Late one night there was an explosion inside the burial chamber that blew the whole damn tomb to hell! Immediately thereafter "El Doctor Loca" left the Keys and was never heard from again."

"My God what a story! It's the stuff that Grade B Hollywood Movies are made from!" I concluded. Hemingway offered no reply. "Papa, you said earlier that you use to love the Keys before they got "fucked up". How did ya mean that and what happened?" I asked.

"Now that's a topic that can truly get me black ass!" Hemingway said with one of his big wide grins. Then, taking a swallow from his large glass of Tom Collins, leaning back in his chair, titling his large head to one side he related that the problems of the Keys; for example uncontrolled expansion and development, dredging, filling in of

78

wetlands with garbage and trash, inadequate public services facilities, etc., "It all began;" Papa started, "with arrival in the Keys of an egotistical, self-serving, loud mouth, conceited son-of-a-bitch named Julius Stone." With this sterling endorsement of Mr. Stone's character, Papa continued on with how in 1934, then Florida Governor, David L. Sholtz had called upon Washington for help as the governor had officially declared the bankrupt Keys a welfare state as jobs for wages were very scarce. By the mid-30's the cigar and sponge industries had both moved to the Tampa Bay Area. The Navy, our continental most southern military symbol in the U.S. since 1832, abandoned its Key West base a century later as did the Coast Guard. Mallory Steamship Lines no longer scheduled stops at the island, and Henry Flagler's Florida East Coast Railroad was in bankruptcy. Its tax base devastated, Key West, once Florida's most affluent city, had sunk five million dollars into debt. The city was unable to pay policemen, fireman, and support other public services. Approximately eighty per cent of residents were on welfare and per capita income was down to seven dollars per month. As southeastern director of the Federal Emergency Relief Administration (FERA), Julius Stone saw an opportunity to be the messiah for Key West and the keys. Again, according to Papa, Stone was self serving, self promoting, power hungry, and ambitious. Thus, while Stone was evaluating his options as to how best to again bring prosperity to the area he gazed out over the azure emerald waters teeming with fish, witnessed the brilliant sunsets over the Gulf of Mexico, saw the bougainvillea in bloom tucked in among unique architecture, and heard the rustle of the trade winds through the coconut palms. Presto! Stone immediately began to cook up Key West and the keys as a tourist resort, a touch of the tropics in a temperate zone. Uninterrupted, Hemingway quickly acknowledged that the area desperately needed to be elevated economically. However, to ensure and maintain the integrity, culture, environment, and pristine of the keys any programs initiated by Stone, so said Hemingway, needed to incorporate "construction with consideration." In lieu of such "consideration" Stone launched his own brand of "progress without pity." That is, Stone secured people to work painting and repairing some homes, buildings, remodeling structures, building thatched huts on the beach, etc. Unfortunately, when 'Stone The Great' sent out a call for 'artists' to come to the 'tropical haven' he had created, many of the local Conchs were replaced on their highway of economic recovery by out of town flimflam and con artists, real estate hustlers, fraudulent land speculators, and deceitful contractors; all who filled the great vacuum created by Stone's free hand and free-wheeling deals. And so the keys began a metamorphosis from an authentic Garden of Eden to a hot humid local populated with quick buck carpetbaggers.

"And what became of Stone?" I asked.

Hemingway managed a smile and related, "The son-of-a-bitch left after several years, got a law degree, returned to Key West and began to practice law; but his shady deals caught up with him and he had to flee the country to avoid prosecution."

"To where did he flee?" I persisted.

"Would you believe I was told the shady bastard is right here in Cuba?" Hemingway concluded shaking his head and now sporting a half smile.

In the years to follow, Hemingway's assessment regarding the impact of poor planning on the future of the Florida Keys and the protecting of its unique beauty and environment would prove catastrophically accurate. If not wholly, then partially, Julius Stone, the Federal Government's paid P. T. Barnum was -- and indeed is---- responsible for the ruination of the turtle and lobster industries in the Keys, the destruction of the once magnificent coral reefs, and the raping of the keys by industrial dredging so as to spew forth irresponsible commercial development. Having personally visited the keys and Key West on numerous occasions over the years I can attest to the fact that it has galvanized itself as a site for vagrants, riffraff, shady realtors, and promoters of scams. Indeed, the Hemingway Days and Hemingway Look-Alike events once endorsed by the surviving members of Hemingway's family and heretofore held at the now debauched Sloppy Joe's has been moved to the West Coast of Florida as a result of avarice commercialization, drunkenness, and aberrant social behavior. Consequently, how ironic that Julius Stone, a power mad Federal bureaucratic should have been sent to the Florida Keys with the mission of planning economic development programs for the local Conchs only, in reality, to have snapped defeat out of the jaws of victory by creating an agenda of disfranchisement for the Conchs but embraced out-of-town profiteers.

As Hemingway terminated his discourse on Key West I stated, "Papa, having seen the film TO HAVE AND HAVE NOT with

Humphrey Bogart and Lauren Bacall, if I close my eyes late at night in a-quite room, I can see Key West, the PILAR, and Sloppy Joe's. Did you see the film?"

"Oh, hell yes! I wanted to see what kind of a job Faulkner (William Faulkner) did in adapting the work to the screen," came the reply.

"And what kind of a job did he do?" I probed.

"First rate; It was good stuff given the Hollywood bullshit he had to put up with. Do you know Faulkner's work?" Hemingway asked.

I acknowledged that I had read Faulkner and enjoyed his works very much.

"Keep on reading him. He's the best goddamn local colorist writing today," Hemingway proclaimed.

"Papa what did you mean when you said Faulkner did a "first rate" job with the screen adaptation in lieu of the Hollywood bullshit?" I probed again.

Hemingway leaned forward in his chair and placed his big forearms on the table and announced, "Writers -- not the screen writers -- do not produce the quality material in Hollywood that they create in their own working environment."

"Why?" I asked.

Hemingway's eyes were fixed on me as he stated, "Because they don't have control over their own material. Shit, ya got directors pulling the writers in one direction, the producers pulling in another direction, the cinematographers in another direction. Everyone involved in the making of a picture is pulling the writer in all different directions; prop men, makeup artist, everyone! Jesus Christ, even the stars give the writers shit! Scott (F. Scott Fitzgerald) told me that when he introduced himself to Joan Crawford on the set of a film the goddamn bitch gave him an icy stare, shouted "Write well or you'll hear from me!" and marched off Hell, Huxley (Aldous Huxley), Scott and some others didn't last in Hollywood as writers adapting works to the screen. Ya gotta remember Shadow; literature can not be transferred to the screen without losing something of its value. Ayn Rand with her FOUNTAINHEAD is the only one I know who ever had and maintained control over her work -- and she never did anything else with Hollywood. Like I said, overall, Faulkner did the best job -- and he eventually left, and he, like poor Scott was a rummy and that only complicated their problems."

"When you said Faulkner did a good job in lieu of the Hollywood bull shit I thought you were talking about HUAC," I intoned.

Hemingway grabbed his glass which had been refilled with a fresh Tom Collins, took a large gulp, leaned back in his chair, and began with, "HUAC verifies Edmund Burke's observation that: All that is necessary for evil to triumph is for good men to stand by and do nothing. Or you might re-phrase Burke and say those who do nothing are as guilty as those who do."

"I think I understand the objective of HUAC. Was it not to root out who the committee members thought were communist?" I inquired.

Hemingway again leaned forward, stared directly into my eyes, and began, "Shadow, objective my ass! There was no objective with HUAC, there was only a committee that had intents and purposes; and ya gotta learn the difference between the two. HUAC's intent was to use Hollywood with some of its screen writers, producers, directors, and stars to achieve their own purpose which was to enhance their own political future and success and get the free public spotlight as well. The HUAC members had naked ambitions and hidden dreams. What they produced were broken lives and shattered careers. To accomplish this HUAC plotted that with any witness, they would classify them as 'Friendly' or 'Unfriendly'. A 'Friendly' witness simply had to deny ever being a communist or communist sympathizer and name someone who they thought might be. The actors George Murphy, Adolph Monjue, Ronald Reagen, Robert Taylor, and George Montgomery were 'Friendly' witnesses. If HUAC decided you were an Unfriendly' witness you could still redeem yourself by admitting you were a communist or communist sympathizer and start naming names of people who you thought might be. It was the old Washington Circus of: Name, Blame, and Shame."

"And what about if you truly believed by answering the committee's questions you were placing yourself in a dangerous position and therefore chose to exercise and protect your constitutional rights?" I innocently asked.

Hemingway smiled; a smile of approval, but masking a bit of annoyance and related, "Many brave and courageous people did just that believing that their rights were protected under the constitution. Shit, that's what Bartley Crum, the attorney for the Hollywood 10 believed and that's what he told them. Obviously it didn't work out that way because when "the 10" refused to answer the HUAC questions or took the Fifth Amendment they were held in contempt. As I said, lives were destroyed and careers shattered."

"Who was the 'jump starter' for HUAC?" I probed.

"A sorry sack of shit named J. Parnell Thomas, Congressman from New Jersey, was Chairman of HUAC," Hemingway related.

"Did you know any of "the 10"? I asked.

"I knew of them, I really don't know them. I can tell you this, they were gifted, talented people who showed great bravery, gallantry, resolution, and who understood and demonstrated the essentials of decency and justice far in excess of the HUAC Inquisition with J. Parnell Thomas as its Thomas de Torquemada. For this courage they -- and others paid the full price," Hemingway affirmed, his voice alternating between a high and low pitch.

"And who were some of the people that were crucified by HUAC?" I inquired. As Hemingway took another gulp from his Tom Collins glass and I a big swallow from my glass of red table wine Hemingway drew in a large breath and began, "Well, there was Dalton Trumbo, a brilliant writer and a valiant soul, who was blacklisted and consequently moved to Mexico. And, there was Ring Launder, Jr., another brilliant writer who was sent to jail on contempt charges as were the screen writers John Howard Lawson, Lester Cole, Samuel Ortiz, and the producer Adrian Scott. Let me think, also charged with contempt were Hurbert Biberman and Paul Jarrico who wrote and produced a great film, SALT OF THE EARTH. Hell, there was Abraham Polonsky and Albert Maltz who likewise received contempt charges. Polonsky and the actor John Garfield did a damn good film BODY AND SOUL that later got Garfield's ass in hot water with HUAC. HUAC said Garfield, because of his association in earlier years with The Theater Group, was a 'commie' sympathizer and that Garfield's wife was definitely a 'commie.' Then, when HU AC called Garfield to testify by giving names and naming names of people he suspected of being "Hollywood Commies," Garfield, as a point of principal refused and told HUAC to essentially go fuck themselves."

"Hell," I interrupted, "I've seen a lot of Garfield's films and I'll be damned if I ever saw anything that was communistic or sympathetic towards the communistic cause. What else were these people supposed to have done and being investigated for?"

"Nothing, other than thinking there was freedom in America and believing in the U.S. Constitution. So, believing that, they refused to answer self-incriminating questions. Hell, according to HUAC Hollywood, TV, and the radio industries were all infiltrated by 'commies' with the consequential result that a lot of well known names were blacklisted and appeared in the publication RED CHANNELS. People like Orson Wells, Lee Grant, Danny Kaye, Shirley Temple, Lucille Ball, Edward G. Robinson, Harry Belafonte, John Henry Faulk, and a whole bunch of others. Faulk got Luis Nizer to sue the owners of AWARE BULLETIN and Ed Morrow of CBS gave Faulk a personal check for $6,000.00 to help out with expenses as Faulk couldn't get any work anywhere. Hell, even his marriage went down the toilet."

"Didn't these people get any support from the industry?" I innocently asked.

Hemingway displayed an expression of contemptuousness and remarked, "Shit, the industries, especially the Hollywood Moguls refused to stand by or give any support to their people and in some cases even turned on them! The worst of the lot was that sad sack of shit Jack Warner who boasted in front of HUAC that he would set up a special fund just to " -- ship 'commies' to Russia! 1 Shadow, it's a historical truism that one is often betrayed by the people they trust the most."

Looking directly into Hemingway's eyes I offered, "All because they chose not to answer loaded questions, betray a friend, or at some point in their past attended an arts festival they were subjected to the ravings of HUAC's committee members who were at the political intersection of stupidity and ignorance. But Jesus Christ -- Shirley Temple -- a communist! That's obviously nonsense!"

Hemingway managed a slight condescending smile and allowed, "You're young, Shadow, so let me line it up for ya. Understand, the obvious is always a deceitful temptation in the arena of practical politics. HUAC knew that by attacking Hollywood and the media with the industries high profile personalities that such assaults would generate worldwide attention; and, their onslaught did just that. From that view, HUAC was successful. Where and when the members of HUAC began to step on their dicks occurred when they failed -- or chose -- to perceive that the line between investigation and persecution is very thin. It was at that point that the news media, along with civil and human rights groups, began to sound the alarm and alert the public that accusations are not proof and that the act of blacklisting denies a person's right of presumed innocence until proven guilty and their right to face their accuser. The news media, along with human rights groups and now some members of congress began asking how America can defend 'liberty and freedom' around the world when we deny it to people at home. Then, the final chapter for HUAC was written when portions of the investigative hearings were filmed and it became clear that HUAC and all its buffoonery would stop at nothing until congress stopped them. Ya see, Shadow, HUAC forgot another important fact and that is TV is an image making tool rather than an instrument of reform. Therefore, is matters of public opinion, the truth is what people think it to be, and with HUAC people saw the committee members as a bunch of ranting, raging madmen. Ya gotta remember other than the personal political ambitions of a politicians, the purpose of a congressional committee hearing -- or any political hearing -- is to send a message."

"And after HUAC and its committee members were brought to a conclusion having shattered lives, destroying careers, and looking like imbeciles were there any apologies forthcoming?" I asked.

"Jesus Christ, Shadow; don't be gullible!" Hemingway intoned.

"Jesus Christ, Papa, HUAC was the aggressor and you said the press and the public realized the committee members acted like idiots. I would think something would have been said as an explanation," I responded.

Taking another swallow from his Tom Collins glass, Hemingway causally offered, "HUAC and its members took the position that they were 'acting in the interest of national security' -- that amorphous entity that permits governments to do anything to anyone at any time. Hell, the committee members were like the thief who is not the least bit sorry for stealing, but is very sorry for going to jail! These fools had their agenda and they saw in the witnesses what they wanted to see -- not what was. If there was one sweet moment it occurred when that sorry sack of shit, J. Parnell Thomas was charged with stealing of public funds and had his dumb ass tossed in jail." I learned that like 'black ass,' 'sorry sack of shit' was a common expression of Hemingway's. Continuing, Hemingway related that, "HUAC never had any justification for persecuting those in screen writing, production, and arts. Still, if the committee had the intelligence and competency to focus on a candidate to question it would have been Charlie Chaplin."

"You mean Chaplin the "little tramp?" I managed.

Hemingway, with his voice rising retorted "Ya goddamn right! That hypocritical, ungrateful bastard had more viable credentials for questioning than anyone around at that time!"

"I've read where Chaplin was a philander and a perverted bastard, but not a communist sympathizer," I commented.

Leaning forward, Hemingway with one palm down on the table and the other wrapped around his glass of Tom Collins stated, "Let me line this up for ya. Chaplin went to San Francisco in the '40s and addresses the members of a conference -- in total sincerity -- as 'comrades.' Later, he professes his support for communism. Then, he expresses his admiration for Joseph Stalin! Stalin -- that butcher of the people."

I interrupted with, "I agree those were dumb statements to make -- especially at that time; but you said Chaplin was hypocritical and ungrateful. In what way?"

"Well, the phony bastard does a film called THE DICTATOR in which he lampoons Hitler, and that's great. Still, how in the hell can you make sport of Hitler as a dictator in one breath and not Stalin in the next. If you're gonna be consistent with dictators and sauce the goose, than ya can't let the gander remain dry now can ya? Jesus Christ, Stalin -- along with Hitler two of this century's greatest mass murders! And let me tell ya another thing. Chaplin comes to America from England without a pot to piss in or a window to throw it out of and makes millions of bucks! That's okay because that's what America is about. However, when the great depression hits with its devastation and consequences, Chaplin refuses to participate in any public programs that have any social redeeming values. How's that for being a comrade and a person of the people? Also, while he continually refused to become an American citizen he never stopped mocking America and its values" Hemingway concluded.

"Ya know Papa, given your known support of the Republicans in Spain and your work with the production of THE SPANISH EARTH, I'm surprised HUAC didn't call you as a witness," I injected.

Hemingway leaned back in his chair with his hand still wrapped around the now half empty glass of Tom Collins and said, "I heard that I was considered as a witness, but it wasn't because of my involvement in Spain, it was because of TO HAVE AND HAVE NOT. There were some who thought it was sympathetic to communism."

"What! Oh, my God, that's bullshit!" I shouted.

Hemingway smiled and replied, "No, my lad, that's politics. Anyway, they never did call me."

As I filled my empty wineglass and conversely drained the carafe of its contents, Hemingway called for Rene to refill the carafe I asked the question, "How was the McCarthy hearings different, if they were, from HUAC's?"

Hemingway wrinkled up his nose and related, "They varied in degree, but not in kind. The variance was the degree of viciousness that McCarthy, his hatchet man Roy Cohn, and members of his staff that include Senator Kennedy's brother Robert undertook with witnesses. Following the opening of each day's hearing, after McCarthy's gang wrapped themselves in the American flag and shouted exaltations, they proceeded to launch a foray upon witnesses that encompassed coercion, intimidation, entrapment, threats, and violated every fiber and thread of human integrity and honor."

"I remember seeing McCarthy on TV and listening to his tirades," I confirmed.

Continuing, Hemingway related that, "In addition to his own personal political ambitions, McCarthy was rude, crude, alcoholic who was a nasty, vulgar drunk and being an egomaniac bullied people to compensate for his own inadequacies. On the other hand, Roy Cohn was a bright, brash, intense and abrasive New Yorker who was use to getting his own way."

"Wasn't that a contradiction of personalities?" I asked.

Hemingway scratched the back of his head and explained, "Well, normally you would think so, but McCarthy needed Cohn. Ya need to understand, Shadow, McCarthy was an Irish Catholic from Wisconsin, the Midwest, and Cohn was a New York Jew. McCarthy like HUAC went after what he called the "left wing liberal Jews" and McCarthy was cunning enough to know that a Mid-west Irish Catholic grilling and interrogating Jews would sound the alarm of anti-Semitism. However, McCarthy reasoned to have one Jew go after another Jew would silence Old Joe's critics. And McCarthy and Cohn, with silent support and backing from the FBI went after what McCarthy called 'pinko' liberal Jews.' Christ, they claimed there were communists everywhere, and they went after innocent people who were U.S. Representatives to the United Nations, worked for Radio Free Europe, and employees of the U.S. Department. of State with malevolence and ferocity. Hell, McCarthy's gang even accused General George Marshall of being a communist and the U.S. Army of harboring communist! And goddamn Eisenhower never raised a finger in defense of Marshall or the Army! Well, after Ed Morrow of CBS did a special on McCarthy and the attorney for the U.S. Army ripped McCarthy a new asshole other members of the Senate shut the drunken bastard down and the rest is history."

Suddenly, Hemingway got up from the table and said, "Be back in a few seconds. Got to take care of my irrigation tool." Hemingway's term for urinating. After returning, Hemingway asked, "Wanna take a dip in the pool?"

I responded, "Thank you, no; but I would like to see the White Tower."

"Sure," Hemingway said. "Let's go!"

Removing ourselves from the chairs, Hemingway charged out of the dining room and I in pursuit. As Hemingway had informed me the previous day regarding the tower, I came into what is the first floor and found the ground level populated with dozens of cats; some in a resting position, some strolling about, one playing with a dead rodent, and nuggets of cat droppings all about. Climbing the stairs behind Hemingway we came to the second floor that contained a bathroom. Continuing the climb we reached the third floor that had a work place and a large collection of military books. Everything about the third floor was intriguing. The work place was built like a podium so that to do any writing one had to stand up and lean a bit forward to write. The military book collection was varied with one outstanding set of works entitled A PHOTOGRAPHIC HISTORY OF THE CIVIL WAR. Finally, the view from the windows was magnificent: sweeping, inclusive, and diverse.

Smiling at Hemingway, I commented, "So this is where you put the proverbial pen to the paper."

"Oh, shit no! Like I told you yesterday I don't do any writing here. After, Mrs. Mary had this built back in '47 I tried to write up here but gave it up."

"Why?" I asked. "It's peaceful and quite up here."

"That's the problem," Hemingway replied. "It's too damn peaceful and too damn quite. I need the activities of the household. Ya know, the dogs and cats about, Lety and Rene with their tasks, the noise of the cooks in the kitchen, the gardener asking his questions, all of La Finca's life in a steady unending movement. That's why I write downstairs."

Hemingway and I stayed up in the tower for what must have been several hours as he related how the early part of the evening was his favorite time to visit the tower – with a full glass in hand. He enjoyed the visits because the view, especially looking to the north, provided a majestic sight with the lights of Havana shimmering in the distance and to the east of the shimmering lights the tiny luminous flickering from the "casitas de los pescadoros" in Cojimar. It was here Hemingway said that during those moments with the placid and calm of the panorama in his sight that he experienced peacefulness and tranquility. We talked about the quietude one can experience when the evening sea breezes carry the alluring fragrance of the tropical foliage and the intoxicating state induced when this experience is blended with a Caribbean moon being embraced by the stars. As we spoke, I recognized a voice calling for Papa from down below to be that of Rene's. Descending the stairway and passing out through the entrance on the first floor, Hemingway excused himself to dispatch some matter that required his attention. I told Hemingway that I would be by the pool area as he went inside. Then, sauntering I made
my way to what was now becoming my favorite chair and moved it between the pool and a large outgrowth of bougainvillea, seated myself comfortably, and began to enjoy what was remaining of the days sunshine.

The calm that had engulfed my mind as it was adrift with thoughts of nothing was interrupted with a high pitched voice that challenged, "Let's see ya wrap a lip lock around this!" It was Papa with a glass in each hand, which I recognized: one his Tom Collins glass and the other a large daiquiri glass which he handed to me. Seating himself in a chair next to me we both observed the birds warping and woofing their way through the bougainvillea followed by a glance at one another wherein we both simultaneously raised our glasses and said "Salud!"

Stretching my legs out in front of me I commented to Hemingway regarding the large volume of military books I had seen on the third floor of the tower. I continued with the question, "Papa, you were witness to, participated in, and wrote about World War I, the Greek-Turkish conflict, the Spanish Civil War, and World War II. If you had to express these experiences in one word what would it be?"

Hemingway remained silent for what seemed like an eternity, but what was in reality but a moment, looking straight ahead, stayed focused on the birds, and then broke the silence with the word, "Illumination!"

"In what way?" I probed.

Hemingway took a sip from his glass and stated, "War is confirmation of the politician's failure to achieve success in crafting the art of statesmanship; and a lot of damn good writers have -- and continue -- to amplify this fact of history. Okay, so this translates out to the reality that each generation will be faced with the task of striving to achieve and preserving peace on a global basis. An enormous task when it is understood that one nation can not stay out of other nation's problems unless that one nation stays out economically. When the economic factor is entered into any political equation followed by physical involvement then the risk of turning regional conflict into global disaster presents itself in a seductive manner. Ya, see, Shadow, this is why it is critical for a nations policy makers to have a full understanding of its leaders intentions and all of the pertinent involved with the intention prior to a conclusive decision to commit to any type of conflict anywhere. In this context, knowledge is not an end to itself, it must have a purpose. And, for a few statesmen wisdom can be terrible when it brings no profit to the wise. For the young of any nation the commitment to conflict is catastrophic because the commitment to conflict says that the emotion of the law of supply and demand is greater than the wisdom of their land. And don't forget that economically, the lives of the young are like currency that politicians are eager to spend for popularity and votes."

Interrupting, I commented that, "I remember my grandfather talking to my father about WWI and how exuberant many of the young were to partake of the conflict; but with their return how their whole perspective had changed; but, hell Papa, you were there!"

Taking a long sip from his glass, Hemingway next took in a deep breath as I had observed was his custom before he undertook a discourse on a topic. Also, stretching out his legs in front of him he began, "WWI was unique in that man's machinery expanded more rapidly than man's ability to control them. Military officers -- and politicians -- did not understand technology. Artillery was responsible for over 50 per cent of the casualties. The machine gun became a scythe of death. Military tactics had not changed for over a 100 years with the result that officers :frequently rose with their troops from the trenches and charged the enemies line with a swagger stick tucked under their arm! It was an industrialized war that claimed over 21 million casualties along with the horror in the trenches where the children of nations came to experience fear, hunger, cold, thirst, disease, and pestilence. Hell, in some trenches if a person was lucky they got to eat rats!"

"Without running the risk of coming across as being patronizing Papa; I experienced a lot of emotion when I read A FARE WELL TO ARMS," I quietly offered.

Hemingway, still focused on the birds responded with, "Hell, I took a stab at what it was like for a young kid to have been exposed to and participated in WWI; but it was only a stab. Now, if you truly want to understand what the experience was like read Remarque (Eric Maria Remarque)."

"ALL QUIET ON THE WESTERN FRONT," I replied.

"That's it!" Hemingway retorted, "There's never been anything since. In point of fact, all works about global conflicts after Remarque are based on ALL QUIET ON THE WESTERN FRONT."

"What about the media?" I asked. "What about the journalists, film makers, photo-journalists in terms of their being able to witness and is some measure experience the madness of conflicts? I'm thinking of the collective media creating an image of an the ordinary soldier traumatized and brutalized by a raging conflict that they do not fully understand and with an expression that cries out, 'See me! Hear me! Listen to me!" I asked.

Hemingway stopped the movement of his glass and held it near his chest which had heretofore been on his knee awaiting a one way journey to his mouth and remarked, "That's not bad, Shadow, ya should write about it!"

"Seriously, Papa, other than literary, the items I recall most about WWI are the posters of the "American Doughboy" and the music of John Philip Sousa," I related.

"Shit, I can't stand Sousa!" Hemingway pronounced. Then, wiggling his big physical form more comfortably in the chair, taking another swallow from his glass, he shared, "I understand what your driving at Shadow. On a broad scale, WWI, as I said before, revolutionized the machinery of death. And while this was occurring and the Angel of Death was reaping a great harvest, the war was being 'sanitized' by our government with the prohibiting of photos showing the hideousness of the trenches and the carnage produced by the new weapons. It wasn't until after the war when the truth came out about the terror of the trenches and the technological slaughter created by the new weapons that people realized they had been lied to. As a result, an isolationism developed as a reaction to what people now saw, read, and heard."

"And the Spanish Civil War?" I inquired.

"Initially because of Spain's geographical location the European media picked up on the political disarray and early violence initiated by the Nationalists. Some American publications then picked up on these reports. But, ya, gotta remember America's economic throat was being strangled by the depression and the 'average Joe' was in a struggle for survival. Also, there were some who remembered WWI -- and some who chose not to -- and from their perspective Spain's troubles were internal and was of no concern to America. For the American media, the 'coin of the realm' was the depression which only served to solidify support for isolationism. Even when Spain's troubles spiraled upwards and became elevated from periodic violent conflicts to open civil war the media coverage was restrained and failed to detail that Spain's Civil War -- like most civil wars -- had fresh unsympathetic savagery, and it was a conflict which utilized on both sides on a large scale civilians as part of an attack because they were part of a countries ability to wage war; but, hell, by '39 Spain's Civil War was out of control," Hemingway stated.

"You gave coverage and highlighted what was happening in Spain." I replied.

"Now get it straight, Shadow. I sent back dispatches for NANA (North American Newspaper Alliance), but there were a hell of a lot of others who did so in addition to speaking out, writing, and calling attention to what was going on. There was Hellman (Lillian Hellman), Lardner (James Lardner, son of Ring Lardner), Wells (H. G. Wells); and others; all who made the effort with their coverage -- and courage to alert the world as to what was truly happening in Spain and what it would mean to the future. But shit, the efforts were exposed to eyes that were blind, ears that were deaf and minds that were closed," Hemingway said remorsefully.

"You did THE SPANISH EARTH and FOR WHOM THE BELL TOLLS!" I submitted.

"Ya, there was THE SPANISH EARTH," Hemingway intoned -- and nothing more. From the conversations of yesterday and now it was clear that the Spanish Civil War was a tender topic for discussion with Hemingway and I explored it no further. Consequently, I moved the talk of world conflict forward in time with the statement that, "WWII certainly had its media coverage!"

"Well, ya, WWII can be looked upon as an extension of Fascist Spain's victory over the Loyalists and the people. Still, other than a few visionaries who intellectually had journeyed into the future and saw what was materializing in Europe, the majority of the American media -- and the American people still supported isolationism. Hell, it wasn't until the bombing of Pearl Harbor that everyone woke up! Then, immediately after Pearl Harbor total media coverage of the war became common place. But, ya gotta keep in mind Shadow, that WWII was different in that the issues were crystal clear: we were attacked; the philosophy of Fascism represented the purity of evil with the leaders of Fascism living out their pathological fantasies and dreams, and their governments composed of living corpuses with dead souls. America's time of innocence and its state of grace was over. Many people now understood that where madness rules the absurd could not be far away. They could see the Fascist in the darkness reaching out to the darkness with their armies of perversity ready to embrace an angry wind."

"I recall Pearl Harbor and the graphic photos in the newspapers," I injected.

Continuing without a major pause except for another swallow from his Tom Collins glass Hemingway went on to expound that from the outset of America's entrance into WWII there was a differential between facts and the news to form public opinion and propaganda.

"In terms of accurate, emotional, and informative coverage Papa, who stands out in your mind as true professionals?" I inquired.

Hemingway squinted his eyes a bit and allowed, "There were many good people, good-eggs who stayed professional; still, Ernie

Pyle, God bless him and old Ed Morrow with his broadcast from England clearly will always rate high with me. Both men shared with the American people that the war would cross the line from inhuman to inhumane with its unspeakable horrors and that while many of the wars participants fully ran the risk of being dead, it was why they died and how they died as variables that impacted on how they lived their lives and how we are to live ours."

"What about yourself, Papa; I can recall my father looking forward to reading the reports you sent to COLLIER'S?" I asked.

"Ah shit, I sent some stuff back to the states but so did a lot of other journalist, like Walton, (Bill Walton with the London Bureau of the LUCE magazines), but the material didn't have the intensity that it had in Spain," Hemingway commented.

"Earlier you said that in WWI, our government 'sanitized' photos and reports that showed the bloodshed and sanguinary of the trenches, was there any such government control on the journalistic material coming out of areas of conflicts in WWII?" I questioned.

"Ya, but the restraints were not directed to subdue the results of the hostilities, they were directed to subdue selected events and personages," Hemingway annotated.

"For example?" I probed.

"To begin with some of us when we got to the continent began to hear about the Nazi concentration camps and what was going on there. When attempts were made to communicate such material back to the states, it was suppressed. When some reports did make their way back -- by one means or another -- they were suppressed stateside. Also, there was the bullshit about our ambassador to England, Joseph Kennedy, who was sympathetic to the Third Reich! Some of the press boys wanted to set the record straight on that son-of-a-bitch, but these attempts were quashed. Then there was that sad sack of shit, the Duke of Windsor who was sympathetic to Hitler and the Third Reich. I get black ass every time I think of him! Ya know, that son-of-a-bitch had the temerity to barge right into La Finca one evening! He never called, never made any arrangements; just came here with his wife! God, what a horrible woman! She pussy whips the hell out of that pathetic wimp -- and I think the dumb bastard likes it!"

Taking an opportunity to be a bit whimsical I remarked, "Of course, I am confident you were the essence of graciousness, hospitality, and diplomacy with the Duke and Duchess of Windsor."

Hemingway, turning towards me responded with a sly smile on his hairy face, "I was polite to those assholes -- not friendly or courteous -- just polite."

Picking up where Hemingway digressed regarding Edward III's fondness for the Third Reich, I asked, "So anything concerning the Duke's association, admiration, or remarks relevant to Berlin that would have been copy for the U.S. Media was censored."

"You got it Shadow! But it just wasn't our government. Hell, we heard about butchery and orgies of death taking place in the Ukraine by the Soviets against not only the Germans but against the Ukrainians themselves. These reports didn't come out until immediately after the WWII was over."

"Why in the hell did the Soviets kill their fellow countryman? They were both fighting a common enemy -- the dark armies of the Reich?" I inquired.

Hemingway paused for a few seconds and explained, "One would think so, but that's not the way it was. When I was in France during the liberation of Paris some of us began to hear dark whispers of beastly atrocities committed against the Ukrainians, and not just by Germans, but by members of a special segment of the Soviet army and by Russian partisans."

"Why? Were the Ukrainians collaborating with the Nazis?" I pried.

Hemingway responded with, "No. But that kindly, gentle looking super paranoiac butcher, Stalin believed that the Ukrainians may have become contaminated by 'western' thoughts and ideas and therefore represented a future and potential danger to the Soviet Union. So he took advantage of the war to eliminate all the Ukrainian resistance fighters who were attempting to repel the Nazis. At that point in the Ukrainians struggle against the armies of the Reich, they know how to fight their own fellow Soviet Citizens. All total during WWII there was probably around five to six million Ukrainians executed collectively by the armies of the Reich, the Soviet army, and Russian partisans. But shit, Stalin did the same thing in Poland when he massacred thousands of Polish Officers who had been fighting the Germans because he thought they could represent a danger to the Soviet Union after the war."

"Jesus Christ! What depravity and evil! And knowing much of this the allies still gave away half of Europe to Stalin after what all those Eastern European had suffered, experienced, and endured!" I entreated.

"Yes we did -- that's politics," Hemingway sighed.

"But in addition to killing their own countrymen the Russian partisans continued to wage guerrilla warfare against the Nazis," I solicited.

"Oh, hell yes! The armies of the Third Reich may have lit the fires of Armageddon on Russian soil, but the partisans quenched those flames with German blood," Hemingway affirmed.

"And all this was suppressed and censored at the time by governments," I implored.

"Not all. The heroic struggle by the Russians and the Soviet army against the Germans was highly promoted and popularized, especially by Stalin," Hemingway mentioned.

"And the Korean War, how much control of the news took place?" I asked.

"Oh, there was fair coverage without a lot of interference by our government. But the issues were not as clear in the Korean conflict as they were in WWII. Then there was the matter of Old Dugout Doug MacArthur and his attempting to set U.S. Foreign Policy which did much to cloud our purpose for being in Korea -- if we ever had any purpose at all! After Old Doug's initial meeting with Truman, MacArthur became like a samurai without a shogun. But more importantly, we tried to wage a war wherein we mortgaged to political vanity the sensitivity we should have had for our troops and failed to provide them with a lucid objective. That political vanity eventually transcended to stupidity," Hemingway explained.

"And how did this vanity transcend to stupidity? I mean, hell, we had just gone through WWII," I questioned.

Pulling himself up in his chair, Hemingway specified, "Through indifference to chance. Indifference to chance in any physical engagement is a vanity for chance favors the prepared combatant. Once we committed to our course of action, void of a compass for logic, America's troops began a long march into darkness. Oh, the combat cameraman recorded our troop's silent cries of compassion, their passionate grief, but it didn't capture their souls experiencing past regrets and future fears, their mental desire to know -- not just believe that what they were about to die for had righteous values. In America the politicians quickly forgot that there were brave men dying -- and for what -- a cloudy ending at something called the 38th parallel? An ending of any kind without a clear beginning is crassness."

"Well, an article I read on the Korean conflict stated that proportionally there were more medals and commissions awarded during the Korean conflict than in previous engagements," I mentioned.

Hemingway responded with a sardonic, "Ya, sure! Get it lined up right Shadow. Medals are like assholes -- everyone's got one! Jesus Christ, the U.S. Department of State even awarded me a medal! And as far as commissions, shit, men don't follow rank -- they follow courage! Remember, nothing solidifies legitimate leadership more for a soldier than the success of his officers."

At this point having a propensity to conclude our conversation of wars and the reporting of same, I opted to inquire of Hemingway, "So this is the illumination you spoke of before?"

Draining what was left of the liquid in his Tom Collins, glass Hemingway looked up towards the stars that were just becoming visible and rejoined, "A nation can not kill the dreams of its children without going unpunished. A nation can not take a generation of its sons and daughters and march them off to war, have them impaired, torn, ripped, brutalized, and traumatized and then tell them it was all somehow a mistake without paying a price; for their blood and courage will exact a terrible vengeance in the future. If a nation forgets what their children did in a war, how they agonized, grieved, and endured, the courage they displayed- and how they died; then the people of that nation lose something individually and as a nation they lose something personally. The resolve to not forgetting is not determined or measured by the number of speeches given, bronze statues erected, granite monuments dedicated, or flags hung out. The resolve is determined by the peace that the children who have been lost paid for with their lives."

Hemingway continued that when conflicts arise how the young frequently see no future, the old can only remember the past, the generals are interested in fighting the battles of the 'last war,' and politicians remain one dimensional thinkers. Moreover, .Hemingway was troubled that America suffered from what he called 'historical amnesia,' and that we as people and the government we elected, fully understood the rapidness with which our world was shrinking and the increased necessity to resolve diverse opinions through dialogue, and not respond by deploying troops throughout the world and functioning as a 'global cop,' then, as a nation we ran a high risk of becoming embroiled in regional and civil conflicts that we do not understand and would not be successful with and the net result of which would only serve to bring our country into disrepute in the eyes of the world. Likewise, Hemingway was deeply concerned over what he termed the 'mechanization of war' which he said he first fully understood in the Spanish Civil War and man's increased ability to destroy his fellow man with increased efficiency. He viewed such abilities, including nuclear weapons, as mankind's abuse and betrayal of scientific technology.

Hemingway's observations about the future would demonstrate themselves to have a chilling accuracy as America in the years to follow would find itself in catastrophic and tragic conflicts which it did not comprehend, failed to understand, and tried to resolve with blind arrogance in lands such as: Vietnam Cambodia, Bosnia, Somalia, and Latin America.

As Hemingway fell silent, still looking at the early evening stars, I stared at him subdued. Suddenly, Hemingway bolted upward from his chair, looked directly at me with his broad smile and inquired, "Ya hungry?"

Startled, I managed a confused, "Ah, sure, I suppose so."

Charging forward Hemingway cautioned, "Let's go this way, around the edge of the pool. Be careful you don't fall on your ass. There are a couple of loose inlays."

Inside La Finca we made our way to the dining room where I once again took my now customary chair. Hemingway, however, in lieu of his sitting directly across from me took a chair at the end of the table to my immediate right and with his back to the doors that led to the outside.

"Hope ya got an appetite! The cooks made some great "Comida Yucateca"! Hemingway announced.

With the passing of a few moments, Rene entered and rolled into the dining room a cart with an array of crockery dishes that emitted a tantalizing aroma and piqued my already healthy carvings. Next, one of the kitchen staff, an oriental woman who I later learned was a cook, and who I had not seen before entered the dining room. In her left hand she carried a carafe of the red table wine, which I had now come

98

to readily enjoy, and placed it in front of me. With her right hand she placed a second carafe in front of
 Hemingway, without ever uttering a word, left. Then, Hemingway took the carafe and filled his glass as did I. Raising his glass and focusing his eyes directly on mine he said in Spanish, "Shadow, se dice en el norte de Espana, "Dime con quien andas y te dire quien eres."

I raised my glass in acknowledgement and we both drank.

Pulling the cart with the magnificently aromatic food between us, Hemingway ordered, "Dig in!"

When our plates were brimming with an assortment of the Yucatan cuisine, Hemingway held forth as to the specifics involved with each dish. In one earthen crockery was a dish called 'puchero' which consisted of chicken, pork, carrots, squash, cabbage, banana chunks, potato and sweet potato with a delicious stock broth garnished with radish, cilantro and Seville orange. In another, Hemingway directing my attention with his index finger, was 'poc-chuc,' a Mayan dish, consisting of thin, tender slices of pork fillet marinated in sour orange and garlic and served with tangy sauce and pickled onions. In yet another earthen crockery was 'pollo pibil' that was composed of chicken pieces marinated in achiote (annato), sour orange, peppercorn, garlic, cumin, salt and pepper, wrapped in banana leaves and baked. Hemingway finished with the notation that 'pollo pibil' when made with pork is called 'cochinita pibil.'

As we consumed the wonderful dishes before us our conversations were diverse, informative, and entertaining. I inquired of Hemingway, "When you put in with the PILAR along the north coast of the Yucatan Peninsula did you visit any of the old Mayan Ruins?"

Casually, Hemingway responded with, "Yea, I got to Mayapan, Kabah, Uxmal, and Chichen Itza. Uxmal had very interesting art carvings and architecture, but Chichen Itza was the golden city for the Mayan. If ya ever get a chance ya should go visit those places."

I further commented with, "I've read where the Mayans were great astronomers and developed an incredibly accurate calendar."

"Well, that was part of their culture. But most of that stargazing imagery bullshit was promulgated by the Carnegie Mesoamerica Project when they established what should have been serious scholarly studies. Instead, once they got set up the members formed a 'good old boys club.' In point of fact, that's what the group was referred to as. 'The Club' and its head pasha was an arrogant ass hole named Sir Eric Thompson. In lieu of becoming unconstrained with the Mayans of the area and learning the Mayan language these galvanized archaeologist after a stroll through the ruins and countryside would mix a drink at sunset, not that I have anything against a drink, and play classical music! The Carneige Mesoamerica Project was eventually shut down in the late '40s and 'The Club' went off to chase butterflies somewhere else. However, it was a Russian gal named Tatiana Proskourlakoff who interacted with the Carneige Mesoamerica Project, but was never a part of 'The Club.' She eventually dispelled the stargazing concept by first immersing herself in the Mayan culture, second learning the Mayan language, and third studying in depth the works of John Lloyd Stephens, who with his party in the early part of the last century first truly explored the Mayan Ruins. Stephens stated that the Mayans were not part of or influenced by any other culture and the carvings on the Mayan monuments were the Mayans speaking for themselves. True 1archaeology, not cocktail archaeology showed that the Mayans were a hell of a lot more than stargazers; they were artists, artisans, architects, and agriculturists. Also, another fact about the Mayans, they were not the peaceful heaven watchers Sir Eric and his bullshiters led people to believe. When the eyes of the Mayans were not transfixed in awe of the moon, plants, and other luminous points in the sky, they riveted their sights on neighbors and waged war. Physically, they may have been short, stumpy little farts, but they were competent warriors who brutalized their prisoners with sacrificial rituals," Hemingway concluded.

"I always associated human offerings with the Aztecs," I injected.

Taking a large swallow of the 'jolly red table wine' Hemingway acknowledged, "Most people do -- and the Aztecs did; still, the Mayans were no pikers when it came to furnishing up people for the ceremonial rites."

"In some accounts I've read the authors accused the Mesoamericans of being 'blood thirsty barbarians, who lusted for carnage,'" I responded. Hemingway, wiggling in his chair promptly retorted with, "Now that's a crock of bullshit and every time I've read or heard that crap I get black ass! The dumb bastards who write that shit forget that at the same time the Mesoamericans were practicing what they believed, the fucking Europeans were implementing the church's inquisition with its employment of the iron maiden, spiked rack, head screw, hot pokers and utilized these holy instruments against children, woman, the old and anyone else who dare to have a new or different idea than those in authority! Are you familiar with the statement, 'Put the question to them?'" Hemingway asked.

"No," I confessed.

"Well it was a statement issued by one in authority in Europe at that time and it gave carte blanche to those asking the questions to get the answers desired anyway they could. Fuck all (another of Hemingway's choice expressions when he spoke with emotion). Heads on spikes were common in Europe and adored the roads and waterways to the castles of kings and queens. If you were of nobility, had court influence or a lot of dough and you were awaiting execution you could secure the services of a skilled executioner who had talent with a sword or ax. If not, your ass could be burned at the stake or be drawn and quartered for public amusement. Hell, when Hernan Cortez landed in Vera Cruz and eventually came face to face with Montezuma, Cortez didn't say, 'We bring you Spanish literature, music, art, sculpture, science, culture, and wisdom.' Shit, Cortez said, 'Monte, I hear you got gold, silver, and riches and I'm gonna to take what I want and there isn't shit ya can do about it!' At the same time Cortez was plundering, he began to systematically rape, butcher, burn, and torture the Aztecs claiming they were infidels while the priest and other representatives of the church stood by watching, blessing -- and praying for their souls! All of this by the so-called Europeans! Shit! The Mesoamericans had no monopoly on brutality!" Hemingway concluded.

It would be years later when I lived in the State of Yucatan, Mexico, married a "Yucateca," and became familiar with many Mayans that I came to understand what Hemingway that evening was explaining to me as we dined. Specifically, that the Mayans are culturally autocephalous; they do not consider or think of themselves as 'Mexicans,' 'Hispanics,' 'Central Americans,' 'Latinos,' or accept confused labels assigned by inept and untutored bureaucrats who so desperately rush to affix upon a people. They are content and proud to be what they are -- Mayans. They are unique with their own language, beliefs, customs, dress, and history. They are a people who do not complicate the obvious in life. They have a great respect and appreciation for the environment; not as a trendy cause or fad, but an abiding belief that has its roots deep in the Mayans great work POPOVUE. They also trust strangers and believe that other people will keep their word -- and that honorable characteristic proved to be fatal to the Mayans -- as it has to so many natives of Mesoamerica,

Banging his right forearm on the dining table, Hemingway bellowed, "Hey, ya wanna go out by the pool for a night cap?"

I responded in the affirmative with, "Sounds good!"

As we made our way from the dining room back to our pool side chairs we did so at a slower pace given the enormous meal and many carafes of wine we had consumed. Taking our customary chairs we were no sooner seated when Rene came out with the familiar glasses: a tall Tom Collins for Hemingway and a large goblet with an 'E. Hemingway Special' daiquiri for me.

As I took a sip from the delicious elixir I inhaled deeply the fresh cool air now permeated with enticing floral fragrances and beheld the night sky canopy above with its luminous bodies. Exhaling I then took another deep breath and heard Hemingway ask, "Ya all right?"

"Yea", I replied, "I'm just enjoying the evening out here. Papa, ya got one hell of a romantic place here -- especially in the evening."

"Yea, well, life requires more for love than a romantic spot," Hemingway remarked.

"For example?" I asked.

Placing his left hand on his stomach and holding his glass with his right hand also atop of his stomach, Hemingway looked at the night sky and perhaps fixed his gaze at a distant star and stated, "When you see the moon, Shadow, it's beautiful, but it's only reflected light. You need the sun to make it beautiful. We, like the moon, need to live off light and lights warmth. Love is our sun. Still, one must be wise and discerning for its a wise individual who can distinguish the difference between loving someone and being in love like the difference between looking at someone you love and hugging someone you love. Only when you hug someone you love do you experience a defining moment. Likewise, a warm person will never take the happiness derived from loving someone for granted. If they do, they eventually are confronted with the task of how to hold on to someone who won't stay. Or, if you've made a mistake, how to get rid of someone who won't go leading to an individual feeling compelled to chase the one who is running away or they themselves running. It's

102

a situation where a person and someone are always together and eternally apart. It creates storms in the heart. I'll tell ya Shadow, love is a gauge of a person's weakness because for an individual in love that love is obvious, and the obvious always a deceitful temptation in the world of practical relationships." "And what about when you love and loose the love?" I questioned. Hemingway, still staring at the sky expressed, "What you truly love you never lose."

"And if the love is taken from you?" I persisted. "That's life's privilege," Hemingway retorted.

"And when a person self sacrifices for love?" I pressed.

Hemingway moved his eyes from the stars and looking straight at me declared, "That's bullshit! Self-sacrifice is easy! Its sacrificing someone you love that puts one to the test."

"Does that fall in the realm of 'primitive love'?" I implored.

"No," Hemingway said, "'Primitive love' is savage emotions."

Chuckling a little I offered, "Then that assessment must apply to the French."

Hemingway taking a swallow from his glass countered with, "No. Love with the French is a game."

"And the Italians?" I implored.

"The Italians! They love with desperation! Hell, they'll murder for love!" Hemingway laughed.

"The Spaniards?" I continued.

"Love is equitable to romance for the Spaniards," Hemingway specified.

"The Cubans?" I solicited.

"The Cubans handle love with passion!" Hemingway proclaimed.

"Christ, Papa, you got love classified geographically and nationally!" I stated.

"Well, what the hell, I've married four times and loved in all those countries!" Hemingway explained with laughter. Then, falling silent for a moment Hemingway managed with a serious effort, "Ya, married four times. Maybe I loved too hard. It's not always clear. But listen up Shadow, I'm gonna share a little allegory with you I heard from an old 'pescadoro' storyteller named Pancho who was selling pescado frito when I once put in at the fishing village of Telchac Puerto on the north part of the Yucatan Peninsula. This is the way 'el viejo' related the tale to me: 'In Mexico, the State of Tabasco teems with vegetation, animal and sea life. Today, just as during the time of the Great Mayan Civilization, many an able farmer and fisherman earns a living from its bountiful land and waters. In startling contrast the State of Compeche, to the northeast, supports very little life of any kind. In fact, so deadly are its waters and so barren its soil, it's reported that iguanas avoid the land. The State of Tabasco thrives because it not only receives water from many tributaries, but it gives waters in return. But since the state of Compeche has no significant outlets, the water merely stays and stagnates."

"People with love are like those two states. Those who receive and give, in return are abundant with happiness of the spirit, but those who receive and never give are doomed to stagnation of the soul."

Many years later my wife Alicia shared with me the same parable which she said had its roots in Yucatan folklore.

Raising his big frame from the chair Hemingway announced, "I got a busy day tomorrow. I'll need to rise earlier than usual. Ya need anything Shadow?" "No thanks. I'm set. I would like to borrow a book." I replied.

Making our way cautiously back from the pool area to La Finca we entered the living room whereupon I immediately went over to a shelf where I had previously seen works by twentieth century writers and selected F. Scott Fitzgerald's THE GREAT GATSBY. In a moment, Hemingway came over and took the volume from my hand and replaced it on the shelf with the comment, "If your gonna read Scott, read his best work," As he selected another volume and handed it to me.

"I thought GATSBY was his best," I remarked.

"It was his most popular work -- not his best. This is his best. There's more of Scott in here than in any of his other works. Let's see if you believe that "The invented life is more important than the real life."

The volume was TENDER IS NIGHT.

"I don't understand, Papa, about "The invented life -- ".What does it mean?" I asked.

"Read the book!" Hemingway instructed.

Looking at the book I remarked to Hemingway, "Fitzgerald must have been a very interesting person. You knew him, right Papa?"

"I'm not sure you ever know what someone is like. You'll never truly get it straight. The only point of reference you have with a person is the past and as time moves forward time tends to put events and images in a problematic perspective. But, let me say this about Scott. Like many Irish writers he had the magic to weave wonderful words into a tapestry of feelings. He could have produced many more great works, but he wasted, and had wasted, a lot of his magic."

"I'm given to understand he had a serious problem with the drink," I commented.

"Oh, hell, he was rummy. He had bottles of hooch stored everywhere and he always had some 'sneaky Pete' in his flask. But the booze was only part of his problem. His wife was the other part of his problem," Hemingway explained.

"That would be Zelda," I specified.

"Yeah, what a bitch!" Hemingway affirmed and continued with, "She tried to compete with Scott on the artistic level with her painting, dancing, and writing. Yeah, she was a real bitch and never liked me worth a shit! So, ya all set? Want anything else?" Hemingway inquired.

"No, Papa, I got everything," I responded.

"Let me get Rene to go with ya to the guest house," Hemingway offered.

"That's OK Papa, I know the way and the lights are on outside," I said.

"Okay then, I'll see ya tomorrow early at breakfast," Hemingway concluded and left me in the living room.

I left La Finca and once outside with Fitzgerald's TENDER IS THE NIGHT clutched in my left hand drew deeply the delicious cool fresh fragrant evening air and made my way to the guesthouse. Inside, I reenacted the previous evening's activities what with the folding of my clothing, storing of the overnight bag, etc. With the putting on of the reading lamp I comfortably positioned myself in bed -- somewhere between the spirits of Marlene Dietrich and Ava Gardner -- and opened TENDER IS THE NIGHT and began seeking the concept of '-- invented lives.'

Approximately an hour had lapsed when I became cognizant of what I believed to be a large number of people in the distance shouting, whooping, and yelling followed by pulsating lively music. I strained to hear some of the dialogue coming over a loud speaker but was unsuccessful as the gathering was too far for me to distinguish as to what the substantiveness of the assembly consisted. Back to TENDER IS THE NIGHT. I read for perhaps an additional forty minutes whereupon with my eyes becoming heavy I left Dick Driver in Paris, put the book down, turned off the lamp for what I thought would be a few moments to close my tired eyes. While I did not uncover that evening the meaning of' -- invented lives,' I came to realize that, indeed, TENDER IS THE NIGHT for I succumbed to a slumber swiftly. I had experienced another exhilarating, illuminating -- and tiring day at La Finca Vigia.

Illustrations:

The front gate of La Finca, which faces a rough dusty road in the town of San Francisco de Paula, opens on to a trail that leads up to the terrace and front door of La Finca. The trail is flanked by palm trees.

Built in 1947 by Hemingway's fourth wife, "Miss Mary", the tower of La Finca contains 3 floors. The first floor was the permanent home for over 30 cats, and the second floor held the bathroom. On the third, and final, floor a library of military books, a work place, and a magnificent view. Contrary to popular belief, Hemingway did not sit in front of a typewriter and work on the top floor. He informed the author that the tower was too quiet and that he did most his writing at a desk in his bedroom, in longhand, and used a pencil.

In Key West and Cuba, Hemingway developed an abiding fondness for dogs and cats. This great fondness was reflected when tragedy would occur and Hemingway was moved to activities that included writing a poem to erecting headstones at the animal's grave.

La Finca contained a picturesque array of tropical floral, foliage, and botanical delights that enhanced and complemented its physical structure.

Now empty, the swimming pool of La Finca was utilized by Hemingway for "pleasurable exercise" to help keep his weight under control. Also it was a focal point for celebrities such as Malcolm Cowley, Archibald MacLeish, Arnold Gingrich, etc. to gather. Ava Gardner, according to Hemingway, liked to swim "bare ass". It was at the pool surrounded by bougainvillea and birds that the author enjoyed E. Hemingway Special Daiquiris and Hemingway his Tom Collins while discussing wars, critics, food, and more.

Although the walls of the bathroom of La Finca were in need of restoration, Hemingway prohibited such things due to numerous medical data such as weight variations, blood pressure readings, prescriptions, etc. inscribed on the stucco walls in red ink, pencil, pen, and even carved with a knife.

Still displayed in La Finca is the portrait of Papa and Fidel with individual Championship Trophy awarded at the Hemingway Fishing Tournament that created much controversy among reactionary groups in the US when the photo was published. Many ultra conservatives point to the photo as proof "Hemingway was defiantly a 'pinko' commie." The FBI continued their surveillance of Papa.

Chapter 4
Breakfast, U.S. Department of State, Biographers,
Memorabilia, and Nos Vemos

With true Caribbean character the early morning sun muscled its way through my window and fell fully upon my face. Ah, yes indeed I reflected, yet another miserable day in the tropics! Rising quickly form the bed I washed, packed my clothing and personal items in my overnight bag as my departure today from La Finca had heretofore been discussed with Hemingway. I would leave San Francisco de Paula shortly after breakfast with Juan Pastor in Papa's station wagon for Havana. Initially protesting that I could take the bus back to Habana Vieja Hemingway raised his hand in a gesture of silence and stated that Juan had some matters to attend to in Havana so why not ride along; joking that Juan was a better driver than he, Papa, was. I could not refute the logic. Thus, after completing my packing and checking about one last time for personal items, I began to tidy up the room by wiping out the wash basin, hanging up the damp towel and wet wash cloth, and half-ass making the bed -- clearly not one of my strong points.

Leaving the guest cottage I closed securely the door behind me. Clutching my overnight bag in my right hand and Fitzgerald's TENDER IS THE NIGHT in my left strolled along the path towards 'Casa de Hemingway' and mindful of Lety's previous day's instruction about using the front door, made my way to another entrance of La Finca and entered. Spotting Juan and Rene I smiled and exchanged Buenos dias and headed for the dining room under the assumption that I would surprise Hemingway by being first with a 'taza de cafe.' All wrong! As I walked through the portal there was Papa -- at the head of the table facing me reading a newspaper held in his left hand and his right hand wrapped around a mug of coffee. Looking up he offered, "How ya doing there?"

"Fine, Papa." And as I responded placed my overnight bag in a corner and took a seat next to him. Still reading the newspaper Hemingway asked, "How did ya make out with the 'invented lives?"

I replied with, "I left Dick Driver in Paris and then I crapped out for the night."

Hemingway smiled.

"Oh, before I forget Papa, here's the book," I stated handing the volume to him.

"Keep it!" Hemingway commanded.

"Thank you very much," I acknowledged.

Looking at the empty spot on the table in front of me, Hemingway asked, "Wadda ya want to eat?"

Observing Papa's plate with two fried eggs, a slab of ham, a pile of toast and a large glass of orange juice I answered with, "What you have looks great!"

Picking up a small bell in front of him and to his right Hemingway rang it several times and in a few seconds Rene appeared whereupon Hemingway stated, "El mismo desayuno para el."

While awaiting my cholesterol breakfast I commented to Hemingway, "Papa, as I was walking up here this morning I was reminded about our discussion last evening concerning romance and love. I remembered that wonderful and sensitive section in FOR WHOM THE BELL TOLLS with Robert, Maria, -- and the sleeping bag. Also, I saw the film version with Gary Cooper and Ingrid Bergman and enjoyed their performances. And with Cooper, who I also saw in the film SERGEANT YORK, and who's performance I enjoyed even more. I don't know if it was his artistic gift or the role, but he came across to me as a very sensitive man."

"He is. I know him. I like him, and hunt with him," Hemingway confirmed. "Really?" I blurted in an awkward, almost immature manner.

"Coop is a. conscientious artist who does his homework well. Before production began on SERGEANT YORK Coop went to Tennessee to visit with Alvin York so he could gain a deeper understanding of the backwoodsman who converted to and became an ardent pacifist -- and an authentic American Hero. Coop later related to me that after meeting York and hearing York's beliefs, feelings, and accounts of what he had done in WWI and how it shaped York's views of life, Coop felt humble in the presence of York and left Tennessee a meeker man. Also, before production started on FOR WHOM THE BELL TOLLS Coop spent time with me to acquire an acute perspective into the character composition of Robert Jordan and after I delineated Jordan completely, Coop got all misty eyed," Hemingway stated.

"So he does his homework well, as a professional artist would, and his is genuinely sensitive to boot," I remarked.

"Oh, hell, yes. Coop told me about a get together he, his wife Rocky and daughter Maria had at their home, which, by the way, houses a great firearms collection. Well, among the guest was Judy Garland who at one point during the evening in an impromptu fashion and without any accompaniment began to sing DANNY BOY. Well, Coop said when Garland finished the song there wasn't a dry eye in the house and as for himself, he was a human waterfall. Yeah, old Coop has deep feelings," Papa concluded.

With the arrival of my cholesterol breakfast I related to Hemingway that prior to my dozing off the previous evening I heard music, voices, whooping, shouting, loud speakers in the distance and what was all the ruckus all about. Hemingway responded nonchalantly as he cut his slab of ham, "No doubt a local political rally against the Batista Government. Probably encouraged by the 'veintiseis de julio hombres.'"

"Who?" I asked.

"The 26 of July Men, The Fidelistas," Hemingway answered.

Having lived in the Tampa vicinity I had been aware of the resentment that many of the Cuban residents of the area held and expressed towards Fulgencio Batista's government in Cuba. The dictator ruled the island nation as his own personal kingdom utilizing terror and brutality to loot and plunder Cuba for his own personal gain leaving the land awash in abject poverty, illiteracy, and disease. Now living in Cuba I quickly became sensitive to the political reality that Batista and his government of goons were turning the screws of repression ever more tightly upon the body -- but not the soul or spirit -- of the Cuban people. Clearly, a precursor that the former Caribbean Indian solider was apprehensive about the survival of his government. From what I could deduce there was -- or would be ~- a hint of a coalition between Batista and his thugs and the 'veintiseis de julio hombres.' The conflict would only be concluded with the termination of one group or the other."

"How do you see the Fidelista's chances of success?" I probed.

Taking a bite out of his toast Hemingway explained, "Well, if they get to the sugar cane country of Santa Clara without any serious losses then there won't be much to stop them from getting to Havana. Before that, Batista and his bums will have hauled ass out of Cuba.

Also, it depends on how much more physical support the U.S. is willing to continue with for the Fidelistas."

"Support, what kind of support?" I further probed.

Hemingway, finishing his last slice of toast remarked, "Mostly small combat equipment; arms, ammunition, clothing, medical supplies, radio equipment, stuff of that nature."

Poking my egg yokes with my toast I related to Hemingway an incident I had observed in central Havana. An apparently lone Fidelista armed with hand grenades had attacked a fortified police station and although the attacker was killed -- and undoubtedly knew he would be -- managed to inflict heavy damage to the station with loss of life to its inhabitants.

"And what does that tell ya Shadow?" Hemingway now probed.

"It tells me the attacker was a hell of a brave -- or foolish man.", and retorted with, "What does it tell you?"

Hemingway took a gulp of his coffee and looking straight at me announced, "It tells me that the Fidelistas can win their war."

"You sound confident they will," I stated.

"Let me line it up for ya this way Shadow. Who would ya rather march with -- the army of the government or the army of the people?" Hemingway asked.

"The army of the people," I again responded.

Still looking straight at me Hemingway continued with, "In lieu of his bombast and bluster, Fidel may prove that the poor can initiate and win a revolution. My concern is that when the Fidelistas win, the U.S. doesn't jump the gun and begin imposing restrictions and conditions on the new government. Hell, if we can demonstrate a little patience and flexibility it will be one of the few times that we have actually accepted and worked with a Latin American Government that truly represents the majority of the people. Shit! Look at our history!

"During the Depression years, the Monroe Doctrine, as it has been interpreted and enforced, began to decline and interventionism faded away. In his inaugural message in March of 1933 President Franklin Roosevelt formulated what was going to become a historic new policy -- The Good Neighbor Policy.

"That same year, the Pan-American Conference in Montevideo affirmed the principal of 'non-intervention in the internal affairs of other states.' Cordell Hull signed the Declaration on behalf of the U.S. The following year the Platt Amendment was abrogated and the U.S.

Marines were withdrawn from Haiti and Nicaragua. When President Lazaro Cardenas of Mexico nationalized the American oil companies, there was no U.S. intervention. Those were the years of the Good Neighbor Policy. And for this FDR will always be remembered in Latin America, and his Good Neighbor Policy will always be a point of reference in our relationship North and South.

"During WWII the Good Neighbor Policy paid off well. Except for Chile and Argentina all Latin American countries moved from benevolent neutrality towards active support of the Allies cause, declaring war on the Axis and, as proper allies, supplying raw and strategic materials at reduced prices. Nazism was a real threat, and all sympathies were with the heroic Great Britain and the U.S. participation in the war."

"What changed this policy?" I asked.

Hemingway took another gulp of his coffee and continued with "The beginning of the Cold War. The U.S. self-anointed itself as the world champion against international communism. Foreign policy was determined by rabid anti-communism or what even appeared to be an evaluation of communism. Any government was supported, no matter how dictatorial and repressive, provided it professed anti-communism. It mattered not if personal freedoms were destroyed, human rights were violated, innocent people slaughtered, provided that government professed anti-communism. Many of these dictatorial and repressive governments admired, embraced, protected, and employed ex-Nazis with the approval of our government. And any government would be sabotaged or directly overthrown if suspected of leftist leanings or engaged in social reforms that, might affect the interests of foreign capitalistic enterprises. This time, however, a collective instrument had been created for intervention and the implementation of the old Truman-Acherson and Eisenhower-Dulles administrations. In 1947 the Rio de Janeiro Pact of Reciprocal Assistance was signed, and in 1948 the Organization of the American States (OAS) was created. In 1954, in the Caracas conference of the OAS, Secretary John Foster Dulles was the architect of the resolution that was, in fact, the new version of the Monroe Doctrine.

"Shit, seven of the worst dictators of Latin America signed this 'democratic' declaration. As I told you before, this was the preparation for the condemnation of the Guatemalan regime, involved in some moderate social and economic reforms that might affect the interest of

116

the United Fruit Company, which as I also told you, and had the monopoly on ports, railroads and agricultural exports. In a short time a small army trained and financed by the CIA entered from Nicaragua and took over the Guatemalan government."

As Hemingway was winding down his comments my mind raced through a corridor festooned with repressive brutality and savagery demonstrated by Caribbean and Latin American dictators, adored, supported, financed and supplied by the United States: Chamorro and Anastasio of Nicaragua; Juan Peron of Argentina; Francois Duvalier of Haiti; Generalisimo Rafael Trujillo of Dominican Republic; General Torrijos of Panama; General Alfredo Stroessner of Paraguay -- and so the list continued as our American government embraced these butchers who spoke of freedom,' 'democracy' and God on their lips as they returned our embraces with blood on their hands.

After Hemingway had terminated his synthesized history of U.S. interventionism in Latin America, I posed a question. "Papa, regarding the 26th of July Men, if they are successful in getting rid of Batista, do you think our Department of State Intelligence Group will advise that we back off from any interference until the new government of Cuba becomes cohesive and solidified? For that matter does our Department of State know the whereabouts of the Fidelistas and their movements?"

Hemingway drew in a deep breath and exhaled with, "No. 'State' won't advise and our government won't back off from attempting to interfere in any new Cuban Government. Also, the phrase 'Department of State Intelligence' is a contradiction of terms." Then, folding has hands together and locking his fingers Hemingway stated, "Shadow, let me give ya a *BROWNIE* snapshot of what I'm told by the people who support the 'veintiseis de julio hombres' -- the trabajadodros, the field workers, the fisherman, the cigar rollers, the true Cubanos; not the factory owners or the large land owners who spend a lot of their time in Miami, Key West, and Tampa. The message from them is that the Fidelistas are somewhere between the cattle country of Camaguey and the sugar lands of Santa Clara. Such information to State would be of no concern. State is less interested in the affairs of Hispanic people and more interested in protecting their own ass. They don't let the truth or facts stand in the way of a good cocktail party!

"Listen!" Hemingway instructed. "I know these State boys. They spend their time with special interest groups and individuals, nibbling on hors d' oeuvres, sipping chilled white wine, toasting themselves on their searing brilliance, and belching political platitudes. Their idea of educating themselves on Latin American people consist of passing out and collecting business cards, strolling through a local mercado, attending a few native folk dances, and chatting about how quaint and deliciously savage it all is! State is interested only what is politically popular -- not the truth. In place of making America proud of itself in a foreign land, they use gayety to cushion the pain of their own ignorance and stupidity."

Taking a swallow of my large glass of freshly squeezed orange juice I commented to Hemingway that from my limited exposure with our U.S. Department of State they mirrored an image of elitism. Hemingway smiled, leaned back in his chair and remarked that, "They are so goddamn haughty that arrogance seems like a consolation prize." Then, as he took a large spoonful of lime marmalade related that his total experiences from traveling around the world with our U.S. Department of State demonstrated that, "The U.S. has a genius for appointing the wrong people at the wrong time for the wrong purpose. By so doing these people will ask the wrong questions so they won't get the right answers. I'm telling ya Shadow many of the so-called diplomats that I've met have a natural talent for disaster and a self-righteous stench of a converted sinner. A few I've met had a little modesty, but no humility. For the most part they were barbarians with religion; rogues who went to finishing school. Overall, they do for bullshit what rocks do for Stonehenge. My God, if our Department of State had to shoot a sack of shit, they couldn't hit a smell!"

We both laughed aloud. As I took another gulp and finished my orange juice I related to Hemingway as to how I heard him periodically use interchangeably the terms 'South American' and 'Hispanic' and what, if any, was the difference -- indeed, what is Hispanic?

Hemingway spooned another glob of the lime marmalade and rejoined with "Hispanic is a culture. The Spanish language and the Roman Catholic religion are among the oldest and most important culture bonds that unites Hispanics. A South American could be a Hispanic born in a South American country. Within the Hispanic minority in the U.S. people can represent various national and ethnic origins."

Now sipping my second cup of coffee I expressed to Hemingway as to how many Americans looked down upon Hispanics with suspicion -- especially if the Hispanics roll their R's when they speak and have olive or brown skin. To this Hemingway raised his eyebrows and acknowledged that, "Sadly, Americans tend to judge a person's ability by their skin color. You've heard the degrading expression, "White all right, brown stick around, black get back!" To Americans, all Hispanics are shady shiftless souls who are only good as maids, busboys, baby-sitters and gardeners."

Myself now digging with a spoon into the lime marmalade I implored Hemingway with, "Papa, why does our Department of State promulgate such a sanctimonious foreign policy punctuated with insolence?"

Unclenching his hands and pushing himself back a bit in his chair, Hemingway slowly affirmed, "In tandem with the 'red' paranoia exacerbated by the madness of Joseph McCarthy, our government actually believes that American is an eternal thought in the mind of God. The obvious question never occurs to the politicians -- Which America? The America of hard working labors, the America of struggling farmers, the America of native American Indians, the America of immigrants, the America of industrialist? According to Washington, it's enough for our government in making foreign policy that God reflects upon us and no one else on earth. Therefore, so it is rationalized by our foreign policy makers, all other nations and people -- especially those working for progress, reform, or change must have the image of America's might, majesty -- and terror put before them. Then, the message is lucid to anyone or any nation whose philosophies are contrary to our governments: No one person, on one nation can stand against the might of America. To be one with our government one must obey, serve, abase oneself and grovel at America's feet -- especially if you are a Third World Nation.

Smiling, I expressed, "Ya know Papa I don't disagree with what ya said; still, there are some within our government who would say you are unpatriotic."

Hemingway, continuing to lean back in his chair barked, "Fuck all! The Potomac politicians confuse nationalism and patriotism. I'm a patriot -- not a nationalist. Our world is shrinking and we still have politicians wanting to be nationalist. I've had my full of and seen enough of 'nationalism' in Spain under Franco and in Germany with Herr Dr. Goebbels and his pals. Shadow, this is the way it is. True patriots must always be on guard against the abuses of their government; and if this means kicking a few politicians in their ass, then so be it!"

"And that includes your providing a little comfort to those afflicted by our government?" I remarked.

"That includes my providing a little comfort to those afflicted by our government -- and afflicting some of the comfortable within our government," Hemingway retorted with a grin.

Talking a third cup of coffee from a fresh pot that Rene had placed on the table I commented about Hollywood's endeavors at adopting popular literary works to the screen and television's less than successful efforts in the same area. At this point I mentioned I was aware of Aaron Edward Hotchner's efforts at dramatizing some of Hemingway's works for television, and was interested how he evaluated these efforts, as I understood Hotchner was a close friend. Hemingway continued to flash his big wide grin and asserted, "Shadow, let me line it up for ya right.

"The TV dramatizations have been half-ass. Remember, in television literary facts and accuracy are not important to the management of TV or to the performers -- that's why there are Teleprompters. Still, television has a lot of constraints, so the end product is not the total fault of a would-be writer like Hotch. I accept him. I accept him for what he is. I don't embrace him because often he seems to be what he is not. So he hangs around me and makes a few bucks. He's the pilot fish and I'm the 'tiburon.' Got it? Hell, he'll probably make a shit pot full of money off me after I'm dead!"

Hemingway's words were to prove prophetic, for immediately following Hemingway's death, Hotchner, with great desperation, rushed out a book entitled PAP A HEMINGWAY which contained so many inaccuracies and distortions that Mrs. Mary, Mary Hemingway, attempted unsuccessfully to halt its publication. In the years following Hemingway's death and to the dismay and disgust of Hemingway's close associates, Hotchner, unconvincingly, tried to pass himself off as an 'expert' on Hemingway. To the contrary, in the evaluation by authentic Hemingway authorities wherein genuine literary contributions are viewed with a critical eye, Hotchner's rapaciousness

.in representing himself as the 'final word' on Hemingway has, in their judgment, served only to validate the reality that such actions lack an artistic hero's calm and support a shams resolve for survival. Their adjudication: Secure a moral and professional 'jump start.'

As Hemingway and I were casually consuming our respective breakfast beverages, I related that I was given to understand that there were several university professors who were working on biographies about him. I posed the question: Did he, Hemingway, in fact sanction the projects for any of these people?

"Jesus Christ, no! It's pretty well known how black ass I get with biographers and how I feel about them! Listen!" Hemingway instructed. "I can work with most reporters. They're okay. As a general rule and a group and some of them are truly swell guys. A lot of these folks have covered life's actions and events. They've been to the edge and back, been part of the great river of history, and some have even ventured upon the waters when the river has crested, and wrote well about it. Hell, they've paid their dues! But these college guys -- shit, there's a guy up in Princeton who said he's gonna write in depth about my life! The son of a bitch never met me, spoke with me, met or spoke with any of my children, met or spoke with Mrs. Mary, met or spoke with any members of my family, but this academic asshole is gonna write about my life in depth! I'll tell ya Shadow, biographers are lower than donkey shit. They feed on the pleasures of life while the people they write shit about get indigestion! G. B. S. (George Bernard Shaw) is not one of my favorite people, but he had it right when he said, 'Those who can do; those who can't, teach.'"

Hemingway was referring to Carlos Baker's work: ERNEST HEMINGWAY: A LIFE STORY wherein Baker portrayed Hemingway as a negatively oriented individual who lived a dysfunctional life constructed upon a foundation of selective hypocritical detachment. Likewise, Hemingway is characterized as a hypochondriac given to constant bewailing and whining. Further, Hemingway is represented as socially ungrateful, indifferent, and insensitive. Following Baker's book, Jack Hemingway, Papa's oldest son, in his text MISADVENTURES OF A FLY FISHERMAN stated that the majority of Baker's information came from a Col. Charles T. (Buck) Lanham and Lanham's wife. Lanham, retired military and a dull individual was a Hemingway 'hanger on' who's wife detested Hemingway and found him repulsive. The feeling was mutual.

Eventually, the Lanham's emulated Judas when they betrayed Hemingway's friendship by scurrying off to Baker with private tidbits about Hemingway and tattling about personal events and activities. For his part, Baker responded as a fly to a dung heap by faithfully recording the copious amounts of tattling and babbling gushing from the Lanhams. So impressed was Baker with the Lanham's indiscreet blabbing that Baker dedicated his book, in addition to Baker's wife Dorothy, to good old Buck Lanham!

I shared with Hemingway that I had enjoyed some biographical works and offered, among some others, Carl Sandburg's work on Abraham Lincoln. Hemingway quickly acknowledged Sandburg's efforts as a fine text and modified his initial statement on biographers by clarifying his pronouncement was not directed at serious scholarly works, but at the "vultures who feed off the dead and then dash with desperation to an agent or publisher to 'tell-all' -- whatever the hell that means!"

Again, clutching his hands together Hemingway leaned towards me and explained that, "The run-of-the-mill biographers are prone to lie to the readers about the people they write about, and when they lie they surrender their artistic reality. Ya gotta remember Shadow; most biographers do not deal with a lot of questions because it's not the questions that are indiscreet -- only the answers. What often matters in a person's life is not always the things that happen -- which biographers like -- but also the things that obstinately refuse to happen -- which biographers seldom write about. They take a haughty position with the reader by silently saying, 'Let me answer the question you have before you ask it and give you an answer to the question that you want to ask.' Most biographers ransack the lives of people and select what they want ignoring all else -- like a vacuum cleaner without a bag that sucks things up only to blow them to the wind. They are manipulators governed by ambition of which lives and a typewriter are but tools. In the world of writers they are tack sailors, so when the tide runs out they run aground. True writers seek artistic wisdom within themselves -- biographers within others."

Restraining myself from taking another spoonful of the delicious lime marmalade I related to Hemingway that I read where George Plimpton was undertaking some sort of project about him and was he aware of its contents.

122

Hemingway wrinkled up his nose and brow and rejoined with, "Plimpton! What the hell's a Plimpton? The only Plimpton I've ever heard about is from an old friend of mine, Cowley, (Malcolm Cowley) who was introduced to someone named George Plimpton. Cowley said the guy was a phony son of a bitch who tried to pass himself off as an 'intellectual' and accentuated a phony accent and asked a lot of dumb questions about me! Fuck all, Shadow, I'll tell ya, all kinds of people are using my name!"

Adding a little more cream to my coffee, I presented a question to Hemingway that had been gnawing at me since I first arrived: "Papa, what do you consider your best work to date?"

Hemingway, squinting his eyes, looked directly at me and with a bit of annoyance as if to suggest that I should know the answer affirmed, "ACROSS THE RIVER AND INTO THE TREES."

Somewhat apologetic I probed with, "Why?"

Still squinting Hemingway verified, "I know myself and I'm my own best critic. I know what is good and what shit is. There is more of me in ACROSS THE RIVER AND INTO THE TREES than anything else I've done. I'm aware of what the critics have said, and I don't give a rat's ass. I'll tell ya, I loathe those who resort to immature interpretations of a work. It's not enough that a serious writer can provide entertainment for several hours with a narrative without being suspected of 'significance,' or 'symbolism,' or 'allegories,' or 'social trends.'"

It is of interest to note that while Hemingway considered ACROSS THE RIVER AND INTO THE TREES his finest work up to that period of time, most critics considered it his worst.

"And that transcends to the short story?" I inquired.

"Oh, hell, ya," Hemingway replied. "Now, if ya got something ya wanna say, than the short story is the best way to tell it."

"Well, Papa," I sighed, "in counting up my successes to date, I sure as hell don't need to worry about what the critics are saying about me; which suggest I may not have anything to say!"

Hemingway smiled, belched and bellowed, "Ah, piss off Shadow! Stop the humble pie bullshit! I've only known you for a couple of days, but I can line a few things up about ya! Hell, I know you know something about bay and flat fishing and there is a lot of good material in that area! Ya know Tampa and Ybor City and ya speak Spanish! There's a hell of a lot of good stuff there! Ya know the Columbia Restaurant in Ybor?"

"Ya," I replied. "I swilled down a few 'cervezas frio' in their bar."

"Hell, it's been said by a local historian there, a James Covington, that there were more Latin American Revolutions hatched in the Columbia Restaurant than anywhere else in the U.S.! Again, ya got a lot of good material there and something to say with it!" Hemingway concluded.

Perhaps out of subconscious intimidation or a resolve not to appear as a babbling worshiper I made no reply.

Now leaning back in my chair, I probed, "Papa, earlier when you were talking about biographers, you mentioned that 'True writers seek artistic wisdom within themselves-v-' What did you mean by that?"

Tapping his fingers of his right hand on the table and titling his head a little to the left, Hemingway affirmed, "Readers deserve the equation for truth in a work, regardless of what type of work it is. A segment of the equation is inspiration from personal experiences, however, before a writer can inspire, before a writer can touch, a writer must first connect with the reader. Therefore, to connect a writer must understand WHY to write a story rather than HOW to write a story. Writing is much more than academic pedantries. The art, know the science of storytelling is critical in the connecting process. If a writer will not fear cultivating the truth from words, there is no limit to what can be created. A fear of words makes one distrustful of language. A writer needs to continually pass the boundaries of creative expression. When cultivating to create and make the writing effort a defining work the writer must be more interested in creating form rather than imitating form. Keep it free from excess verbiage contamination. Terse, condensed, compact structure is essential to writing true sentences and ensuring the reader won't become confused. There is genius in simplicity. Any fool can trivialize the monotonous! Good writers know when they have created written words that are true. They know it when the reader feels, understands, appreciates, sympathizes -- connects! I'll give ya one example Shadow. In THE OLD MAN AND THE SEA I attempted to open the readers mind so as to provide them the opportunity to participate in the fishing experiences that the pescadors of Cojimar encounter in their daily lives. If you want a parallel, I wanted to do with my pencil what Dorothea Lange did with her camera."

124

"And always having as your beacon of light the creating of 'one true sentence." I said.

"Always." Hemingway affirmed, He continued with, "A person is an imposture as a writer when they fail to write about the things they hold true. Writing, Shadow, is the ultimate form of expressing personal freedom and provocativeness when writing will create a higher level of final achievement. Call it being consciously creative."

I had for approximately the last fifteen minutes observed Hemingway periodically looking at his watch and took my cue that it was time for me to depart with Juan Pastor for Havana. Therefore, I took the lead with, "Papa, I recall you said you had a full schedule this morning and I've got a few things I want to pick up before I make a quick trip back to the Tampa Bay area so I'll get together with Juan now, if that's okay with you?"

"Ya, Sure, fine." Hemingway acknowledged and then inquired, "What stuffy gotta get to take back to Florida?"

"Oh, some booze, perfumes, cigars stuff like that," I replied.

Quickly getting up from his chair Hemingway instructed, "Follow me!"

Obeying his instruction I followed Hemingway into the living room whereupon he retrieved from a table a box, opened it, and began giving me a series of brochures and informational items that included: AVIS Car Rentals, gift shops, THE SAN SOUCI, liquor stores. With each item he provided a set of specific instructions that included: who to ask for, what type of item to buy, how much to pay for the item, etc... Hemingway went on to relate how over the years he, Mrs. Mary, present and past household employees, friends, and others, prowled the streets and environs of Havana and sought out the best bargains. If they couldn't immediately find good buys they set out to find them in a more casual, less hurried manner, and accordingly, if they couldn't find them thusly they launched a 'hunting party.' That entire aside, Hemingway assured me that the brochures and informational items with the specific instructions associated with the materials would yield me the best possible price for the merchandise.

As I was stuffing the brochures into my overnight bag and attempting to remember names and associate them with specific informational items, I heard Hemingway bark, "Hay, ya meet any nice whores?"

Startled, I stammered with, "Well, I -- I mean I met a few nice young ladies."

"Well, hell!" Hemingway continued, "If they were whores ya would have known it! There are only two kinds of women -- honest and dishonest. Personally, I think any man that has to pay a woman to do any 'irrigating,' (another of Papa's phrases for having sex), isn't worth a shit as a man. That's not to say ya can't have fun and a good time with some nice whores. Ya can have fun with them and still not pay to irrigate!"

Feeling a little awkward I managed a nervous smile and mumbled something about, "Maybe with that experience I'll write more than a few 'true sentences.'

"Hay!" Hemingway retorted. "I've entertained the idea of writing a work about whores myself"

Reaching into the box from which he retrieved all the brochures and informational pieces Hemingway took out several cards and handed them to me. They were business cards advertising houses of prostitution. Taking the cards uneasily I made a feeble attempt at humor with, "Ya don't need these?"

Smiling, Hemingway explained, "Hell no! A good friend of mine gave them to me. Said he took the gals out for some drinks, fun, and had a hell of a time."

More relaxed, I responded with, "Obviously, the friend is not a biographer or critic."

"Winston!" Hemingway casually remarked. "Hell, no. He's a professional sportsman."

Curious and half-joking I probed, "Any relation to Winston Churchill?"

Hemingway, without the blink of an eye answered, "Ya, his cousin, Winston

Frederick Churchill Guest."

A bit bewildered, I simply acknowledged with, "Oh."

As we were leaving the living room Hemingway called to Juan Pastor to bring the station wagon to the front and to take my overnight bag. Walking out the front door of La Finca and down the steps that led to the pathway to where Juan was now waiting for me with the passenger's side of the door open, Hemingway and I were engaged in small talk about the weather, the noise of the animals, etc. I was approximately four feet in front of Hemingway when we reached the station wagon and stopped. I turned around and Hemingway was smiling with his big hand extended out for mine. Instead of a hand shake I gave Hemingway an abrazo apertado, the traditional and customary Latin American hug and embrace of affection. Hemingway was momentarily startled, and then responded in kind. Releasing my clasp, I looked at Hemingway warmly and stated, "Papa, don't know how to thank you for all your generous hospitality."

Hemingway still smiling replied· with, "Shadow, time will solve that mystery."

I entered the station wagon and left. I never saw Hemingway again.

Illustrations:

Restlessly roaming the streets, avenues, and boulevards of Havana with their many shops, stores, and emporiums, Hemingway would ferret out the "best possible price for the booze and such". This brochure, given by Hemingway to the author, represented, "the best damn price for hooch in Havana."

Prostitutes were a source of interest and amusement for Hemingway and he told the author that he might – "write a book about them one day." The "Professional" Business Cards, given to Hemingway by his friend Winston Fredrick Churchill, were subsequently provided by Papa to the author with the understanding that the author may wish to – "meet some nice gals and have some fun."

The author with his friend Ernest Hemingway shortly before the author departed for Havana after his weekend visit at La Finca Vigia. The photo was taken by Papa's "unofficial" official manager of La Finca, Juan Pastor. The author and Papa had just exchanged an "abrazo apretado", and traditional and customary Hispanic hug of affection.

Havana's Enchanting
International Favorite!

Havana Nights
With Continental Flair!

ocated in a tropical garden estate in Havana's Country Club Section, away from the bright lights of the city, is the Sans Souci nightclub . . . favorite rendezvous of Havana's elite.

HAVANA'S celebrated Night Club and Casino, Sans Souci, has for you an evening of lavish entertainment . . . finest of foods and cocktails . . . exciting games for stake . . .

Consult Your Travel Agent

Consult Your Travel Agent

"SANS COUCI has the best damn entertainment in Havana!!" so asserted Hemingway when he gave the author this informational flyer.

Besides the glamour of the Casino ... two Spectacular Revues nightly, no two alike, feature not only the most outstanding entertainers in the world, but are supported by a company of fifty to two hundred talented, breathtakingly-costumed performers.

SANS SOUCI

There's spirited Gambling for you ... Start early, every night at 8:30 p.m. with fast-and-friendly "get-acquainted" bingo to win Lady Luck to your side.

Although claiming he was not a serious "aficionado" of gambling, Hemingway told the author he periodically did go to SANS SOUCI to – "take in a couple of the shows."

Sans Souci

You'll feel the warmth and elegance of a private club as you pass through the stately entrance of Sans Souci and join the genial cosmopolitan guests.

In the spacious Casino there's a care-free spirit where light or serious gambling, always under government supervision, is an exciting challenge to your skill . . . and luck.

Johnnie Ray

Ilona Massey

Joni James

Tony Martin

From your table in the air-conditioned dining room or in the outdoor garden, you see the most popular artists in the world today in a lavish revue . . . you enjoy the sheer luxury of perfect, potent cocktails and a delicious dinner in this magic atmosphere.

Presenting for your pleasure the most famous names in the Entertainment World.

133

merican-managed, the services at Sans Souci are unexcelled . . . pleasant and attentive. Even the finest beverages and the delectable international cuisine are prepared by a selected staff . . .

And there is NO cover charge.

Open the Year Around

Here, in the Gay Nevada Cocktail Lounge, is continuous, but unobtrusive, entertainment all evening long . . . a comfortable, softly lighted place to suit a quiet mood.

Thrilling cockfights every night!

Everybody enjoys Bingo at Sans Souci. You will want to try for the many prizes ranging in value from $100.00 to $15,000 nightly. At left, winner receiving second prize of $10,000.

troll in the starlit night through the sweet-scented, romantic gardens that surround Sans Souci. Dance outdoors beneath a Latin moon to the languid music of two top orchestras.

Brilliantly staged outdoors on multi-level platforms in a magnificent jungle of foliage, the Sans Souci extravaganza holds you spellbound. You feel the intensity, the rhythm . . . sometimes pagan, but always beautiful . . . of the original acts which are created to please and thrill you.

Telephones:
BO 7979
BO 8558

Member of the Diners Club

Johnny Mathis

Diahann Carroll

Robert Merrill

Dorothy Dandridge

Helen Traubel

Edith Piaf

Papa gave the author the author Charles Baudelaire's volume of
FLOWERS OF EVIL with acknowledgement that Baudelaire's works
– "were like a ghost without sleeves." The author never liked ghost
stories.

Chapter 5
Reflections: Ghost of a Weekend Past--The Ancient Future

I had come to Cuba in the summer of 1958 determined to secure and acquire material for a written project, which my agenda reflected I would conclude within a twelve-month period of time. Now, over half a century later, the project is completed, albeit not the same agenda I initially began with.

Prior to being a weekend guest at La Finca Vigia, I had read much and understood little concerning Hemingway, the confident twentieth century literary genius and enigma who in his• lifetime moved from fame, to legend, to myth. After my defining weekend experience I came to comprehend more lucidly and to put into focus more acutely a man who was sensitive, sympathetic and a distinguished artist who made important and original contributions to literary history.

Like the corrientes del golfo that Hemingway roamed for years, so Hemingway's life contained many currents of which three flowed, rose, and ebbed most tumultuously.

First, was his passion to engage completely in, and encounter richly, the ecstasies and tragedies of life.

Second, was the competency to evaluate these encounters and record them faithfully on paper. Hemingway created consciously and therefore his writing was an extension of his life. Consequently, Hemingway believed that a separation of one from the other would prove destructive, and, as a stylistic genius, he chased throughout his life a fatal vision of perfection in his writing.

Third, was Hemingway the intensely private man who became fiercely defensive when anyone -- family, friend, or foe attempted to breach the self imposed fortification that he constructed around himself. For those who attempted by design or innocence to scale these ramparts there was Hemingway's swift wrath to meet them as many a-would-be biographer, critic, and associate discovered. Hemingway was fifty nine years of age when I met him. He was married to Mary, his fourth wife, had been exposed to artillery fire in three wars, and restlessly roved the world -- stomping the Upper Peninsula of Michigan, pursuing the great bill fish in the Gulf Stream, stalking for big game in Africa, following the bulls in Spain. From this cornucopia of living experiences flowed his masterful short stories and such works as THE SUN ALSO RISES, TO HAVE AND HAVE NOT, and THE OLD MAN AND THE SEA. Hemingway's work brought to literature a unique style of writing -- terse, realistic, staccato, direct -- a lyrical approach that influenced writers the world over and spawned many imitators; e.g. Norman Mailer.

Hemingway labored with total commitment when he was writing, and when he was not writing he applied the art of relaxation with equal devotion. He understood the necessity of moderating one's self with time so as to relish the pleasures of its environment. He had been nearly everywhere and had digested almost all there was to consume about the locales he had been to. His knowledge of lands, climates, its people and their customs, history and infrastructure was portentous and he held forth on any -- or all -- of these topics routinely and cheerfully.

His focus on his immediate surroundings when undertaking the shortest jaunt slowed his reaching his objective; though for him it was pleasurable. He liked to stop for a taza de cofe or a cerveza fria along the way, eat some fresh fruit at the local mercado, mingle with people, soak up the impressions that would eventually be reflected in his writings. Papa was always more interested in the journey than the destination. While his commitment to his writing was a part of Hemingway the public never observed, it was the most significant part of the 'Hemingway equation.' Writing was a laborious task, invigorating, yet, commanding all from him as he tested the boundaries of creative expression. When he had a work underway, he was completely immersed by it and at the conclusion of each day he would tally the number of words he had inscribed and enter them in a journal.

He related to me that he rose with 'the first rays of the sun' and began the day reading what he had written previously and then editing. Also, he told me that he had rewrote the ending of A FARE WELL TO ARMS over thirty times in manuscript form and worked it over thirty times in proof-- "to get it right."

To venture where one has not ventured, to confront eternity on a regular bases, to attain that which is unattainable -- these qualities demand valor of the supreme magnitude. Hemingway possessed these. Papa always enjoyed a clandestine romance with dangers. For him a formal courtship with life lacked the pleasures of the illicit.

Out of high school at the age of eighteen and a Red Cross Volunteer in the Italian trenches near the Piave River during World War I an Austrian bombardment found its mark killing several Italian infantrymen and shattering Hemingway's right leg. Nevertheless, Hemingway lifted one of the Italians onto his back and carried the soldier across a field amid machinegun fire.

Hemingway flirted with the angel of death on numerous occasions in the Spanish Civil War and during World War II in France as a war correspondent for COLLIER'S, where he soon abandoned that role for active combat with French freedom fighters. These flirtations extended from the battlefields of world conflicts to the fly bridge of his beloved PILAR when Papa would smash the bow of the vessel through turbulent seas in violent storms in the corrientes de golfo, or with his feet planted securely upon the soil of the Serengeti Plain with the sights of his rifle fixed on a charging lion. Still, in lieu of his fearless adventures, and his formidable exterior appearance, Papa was a modest and a tender man. His voice could fatigue and become taut while engaged in unstructured conversations. He rarely spoke publicly because of his acute timidity and when he won the Noble Prize for literature his humble acceptance speech was read in Stockholm by the U.S. Ambassador to Sweden.

This bashful, sensitive side of Papa was seen only by his friends, towards whom he was infinitely abundant with his money, his possessions, and his time -- which to him was more valuable than anything. To this, I can attest. Many were the pescadoros when experiencing 'mala suerte' who with their families, had food on the table and cloths on their backs because of Hemingway. Many were the pescadoros when they set out upon the corrientes de golfo did so in crafts bought and paid for by Papa. Many were the friends down on their luck who received regular sums from Hemingway.

With his rugged good looks, his reserved strength and primitive magnetism, his eager inquisitiveness about everything and everybody, his glow and humor, Hemingway cultivated a charismatic personality in addition to a propensity for friendship that endeared him to many. Arriving in Paris in his early twenties, hardly had he unpacked when he fostered fruitful associations with some of the most advanced literary and artistic personalities of their period: Andre Masson, James Joyce, Ezra Pound, Gertrude Stein, Joan Miro, Pablo Picasso. Meanwhile, within the time horizon of his own generation he

138

governed a nucleus consisting of such talented entities as Archibald McLish, F. Scott Fitzgerald, John Dos Passos, Gerald and Sara Murphy. In the following years and other lands, (e.g. Spain, Key West, Cuba) there would be tied long knots in the line of life with such people as his legendary editor at Scribner's, Maxwell Perkins; celebrities like Gary Cooper and Ava Gardner; sportsman and cousin of Winston Churchill, Winston Guest; correspondent Malcolm Cowley.

Nevertheless, Hemingway's level of expectation of fraternity was demanding and the bar was periodically raised. With one of these levels was clearly his qualification that his friends are people who held together under the most adverse conditions. This absolute fidelity was what Papa valued above all, to be given and to be received, and it was a common denominator to all those with whom he had long and lasting relations. Consequently, acknowledging the parameters that Hemingway established it is not startling that the fatality rates among his friendships were high.

Like the corrientes del golfo which Papa loved, the tide of life carried Hemingway to world fame, but he did not rest upon his ores but continued to row the sea of life that eventually moved him into the misty realm of myth. Throughout his life Hemingway was ready to defend a worthwhile cause with great enthusiasm and warmth.

He felt a strong sense of solidarity with the entire human race, and he practiced what he preached concerning justice and courage. It is acknowledged that he relished conflict, and that adventure and turbulence all played an important part in his life; but he did not rush indiscriminately to any war front just for the pleasure of wielding a firearm, going hungry and feeling cold. "No man is an island unto himself"

Hemingway was a man amongst men. He sometimes made the wrong choice, but he had the courage to take sides because fundamentally he loved his fellow man. He loved the places where human beings congregate. It would be interesting to know how many hours he spent sitting in LA FLORIDITA. Today many people go there on a literary pilgrimage. They sit near his empty stool and ask for a daiquiri bitter, no sugar and a double portion of rum, which was what Hemingway always ordered. It was the right drink in the right place for that sort of man for Hemingway as a subject is not simply an individual, but a finely textured way of life, an era.

After Hemingway's death, La Finca Vigia became a national museum, Museo de Hemingway, and fittingly Roberto Herrera Sotolongo was its first caretaker. He was a Spanish exile living in Cuba who was Hemingway's personal secretary for over twenty years. Later, when Roberto Sotolongo completed his medical studies in Havana, which had been cut short by the Spanish Civil War, Gladys Rodriquez Ferrero became director of Museo de Hemingway.

Hemingway's home at La Finca Vigia has been preserved exactly as in the days when he lived there and remains a vivid moving evocation of the author's life, which this work has attempted to convey. Hemingway lived there for most of his last twenty-two years of his life, and it was the only settled permanent residence of his adult life. It is as if the man might walk into the room of down the path to the pool at any moment. Now, after over forty years as I again stroll about La Finca I recall many of Papa's words and conversations. Some were humorous and funny, others sage and provocative, many were instructive and edifying, a few critical, a lot expectably and confident, additionally some were bitter, but always interesting.

Treading the pathways among the foliage, fruit, and vegetables I came upon the headstones erected by Papa and marking the gravesites of his most beloved cats and dogs. I was reminded of a comment Hemingway made to me when we stopped our evening walk for a brief moment at one of the gravesites. "Shadow, with animals you get and have reliability because no matter how miserable of a time or bad of a day you've had, when ya get home and greet the cats, they purr with contentment and when ya greet the dogs they wag their tails with happiness."

Walking over to where Hemingway's beloved PILAR is permanently on view from heretofore Cojimar, and I, still lamenting the fact that I never did get to go aboard the vessel, recalled an affirmation Hemingway made when we were discussing THE OLD MAN AND THE SEA wherein Hemingway stated, "The sea is a peaceful sanctuary as well as a battleground and it's to the sea that a man goes to find himself.

Standing by the now empty swimming pool where the birds still frolic amongst the landscaping I see the area where Hemingway and I rested comfortably in our chairs enjoying the balmy tranquil tropical evenings. I, sipping and savoring, my 'E. Hemingway Special' and

Papa whittling away at the contents of his Tom Collins glass and I recollect a self assessed statement Hemingway made.

"Ya know, Shadow. I spent my life working at being what I am."

Responding, I asked, "Was it worth it?"

Scratching his leg Hemingway replied, "I'm not sure. Often you can be in the middle of plenty and still be alone with the beating of your heart. The answer to that question is still marinating."

"Papa," I said, "that comment sounds like it carries with it a slight religious overtone and some detractors would say you come across like an atheistic who believes in God! So with what do you respond?"

Hemingway leaned forward, smiled, and in an unvarnished manner stated, "I would tell them to fuck off and stop trying to play God -- it only makes atheism more attractive!"

"Do you believe in God?" I risked.

Looking straight ahead Hemingway answered, "Let's say I believe in the order of the universe, the balance of nature, and the brotherhood of mankind."

"Then you believe in God," I replied.

Hemingway still looking ahead smiled gently and offered, "If you say so."

I said no more.

Climbing the steps of the front terrace and passing through the front door of La Finca, I slowly journeyed the hallway and coming into the living room saw the shelves of books from where Hemingway had selected Markham's WEST WITH THE NIGHT and Fitzgerald's TENDER IS THE NIGHT. Next, I observed the chair that I was guided to by Papa and recognized the 'libation' cart upon which rested the bottle of OLD GRAND DAD from which Hemingway poured me a full glass of 'body warmer' as an introduction to my first morning at La Finca. Then, I retraced a conversation wherein Hemingway laced the art and science of fishing into the challenges of life. He related, "There are some things one does well or else not at all; and if one isn't sure one can do them properly, it's better to give up the fight before it starts. Now, here, consider again fishing. You have your trusted Tycoon bamboo fishing rod and Fin-Nor reel and you tie a line to the outriggers in the waters of the Gulf and run into a marlin that you secured with your hook rigging. Now you will have to put up a great fight with your rod and reel, without cheating, using your own strength and endurance alone. What counts is the fight, however wearisome it grows. Never mind if it lasts form morning till night, pushing you to the limits of your strength. Only when you have won that battle with yourself will you perhaps catch a glimpse of who you truly are."

Proceeding pass the bathroom I monetarily paused, peeked in and recognized the scale in the comer, next to and left of, the douche and the wall to the immediate right with dates, weights, and notations. It was a private place where Hemingway, somewhat of a hypochondriac, would go to 'watch his health.'

Moving from the bathroom doorway and backtracking down the hallway I moved to the entrance of the dining room, entered, and walked over to where 'my chair' was neatly positioned up against the table. I placed my hands on the back of the chair and cast a long glance about the room. It was as if l had left La Finca only yesterday. The heads of the two-prong horns or American antelopes continue to decorate the wall with the side entrance leading to the outside. Mrs., Mary's two French reflecting lamps are on the tables as are the silver ware with the emblem of Finca Vigia. Upon closing my eyes and inhaling deeply I could once again experience the savory aroma of the exquisite and delectable foods that I enjoyed from the kitchen of La Finca and created from Papa's collected recipes. Like; pollo pibil, sopa de lima, poc-chuc, panuchos, frijol con puerco, and, of course, seas of red table wine. Looking over at 'Papa's chair' I was reminded of a particularly warm dialogue Hemingway and I engaged in which focused on the innate goodness of people universally -- politicians aside -- and how he believed that such merit would sustain mankind when challenged by and with adversity. I had remarked to Hemingway, in a half humorous fashion, if he had a specific date for Armageddon, given the stockpile of thermonuclear weapons by many nations. Papa titled his head a bit to the left and shared, "Shadow, since WWII and Korea our present western civilizations are not an exclusive club -- they are for everyone and require a little indulgence and patience on the part of all members. Hell, when we take one step towards understanding others, wisdom takes ten steps towards us because we are all citizens of humanity."

Exiting out of the dining room and lulling a few moments in front of what served as Papa's office and library I saw on the right side of the entrance the plate by Picasso, decorated with a bull's head in relief, which Papa and Mrs. Mary acquired in 1957. On the same wall I saw the other bull's head, made in wicker and bought in Spain. The magnificent desk, so Hemingway informed me, was made from Majagua, a precious wood from Cuba, and was the work of a regional cabinetmaker Francisco Pasos Castro. On the left side of the entrance still remained a Ruano Llopis poster announcing a bullfight at San Sebastian in 1927. Scattered about were African amulets and ritual objects collected by Hemingway, important items for the practicing of santeros. As with all rooms in La Finca, there remained an abundance of books.

Slowly shuffling towards the front of the hallway as you enter from La Finca's front door, I hesitated for a moment and retraced an incident in which Hemingway gave me an information piece on, at that time, the world famous SANS SOUCI. Papa was about to open the front door when he stopped and looking directly at me asked, "Ya like live-shows, live-entertainment, or gambling?" I answered that I enjoyed live-performances, but was no gambler, and even if I were, I couldn't afford to gamble. Then, Hemingway instructed, "Wait here a second!" and dashed into the living room and returned quickly with an information piece of SAN SOUCI in one hand that he gave to me with the notation that, "SANS SOUCI has the best damn live entertainment in Havana and at the best damn prices!" I visited the facility once to watch a show and observe people gambling. In his other hand Hemingway handed me a small volume entitled FLOWERS OF EVIL by Charles Baudelaire with the comment, "Don't know if you're familiar with or like the French 'decadents.' Many of them wrote on artificial and unconventional subjects and used a subtilized style. Baudelaire was one of the best. When he wrote his work reflected a ghost pointing an empty sleeve."

I have read the volume of Baudelaire that Papa gave me several times and my last reaction was as my first -- I don't like ghost. Partially circumnavigating La Finca, I was at the front of the 'white tower' and after passing through the door and climbing the stairs I reached the top, paused, and allowed my eyes to drift from side to side taking in the still resplendent and commanding view. As I did so I was reminded of a somber conversation Hemingway and I had late one afternoon while overlooking the "pueblos" from the tower. It was initiated when Hemingway asked, "Shadow, ya know what's out there?"

"A grand view teeming with life!" I eagerly replied.

Expressing a sad smile Hemingway countered with, "Death is out there. Death with all its surliness patiently waits."

As Hemingway spoke I instantly reflected back to his assessment of death in THE SNOWS OF KILIMANJARO. Scratching the back of my neck, I expressed, "Well, no doubt there are many who think life is written in its final form, when, in reality its only a rough draft."

Hemingway rejoined, "Sadly, I'm sure there is a hell of a lot of people who exist with that concept. But ya gotta remember there's an ocean of difference between existing and living."

Looking out from the tower I specified, "Even if some don't fully believe in life being in a final form, it probably gives them some comfort." Hemingway stepped a little closer to me and affirmed, "Bullshit! When ya believe in things ya don't understand, ya suffer! Consequently, it is easier to die in a world ya understand than live on in one ya don't. Let me line it up for ya Shadow from a different angle. It is better to die once than to live a life in fear of death -- regardless of a person's belief Hell, it's better to die for something than to live for nothing! A good death for a good reason is better than a bad conscience! To that end, a man lives freely only by his readiness to die and with that he can only be destroyed by his own hand!"

I slowly turned from looking out the tower's window and focusing on Hemingway expressed, "And what of those who are suffering with terminal illnesses?"

Hemingway still standing near me explained, "Delaying death is not to be confused with improving the quality of life. Death may be simpler than life and infinitely kinder."

Listening to Hemingway speak of death it was as if his soul were tethered to his being by a thin thread of fatalism. As Carlos' taxi passes through the white gates of La Finca Vigia and makes a turn on the road leading back to Havana, this day, as in 1958, is a transforming and defining experience for me. I recall the man I met that weekend and assess the public image of one of America's greatest prose stylists whose lifestyle has managed to propel him into the realm of myth. The solitary constant remaining was that in 1958 -- as now -- I have chosen to view life as a rough draft. Positioning myself comfortably in the taxi's back seat while Alicia is busy checking a phone number in her address book, I close my eyes briefly and continue to reflect when I was awakened by hearing Carlos asking, "Shall we return to the Hotel Vedado?"

I looked over at Alicia and replied, "Hell no! Let's all go to EL FLORIDITA -- I wanna have an 'E. Hemingway Special!

Nos vemos, Papa!

Immediately upon entering Havana in January, 1959 Fidel began lubricating his propaganda machine by defacing the walls of the magnificent "Malecon" with graffiti proclaiming "26 Julio" (26th of July) – the date that marks the landing of the Fidelistas at the east end of Cuba and, symbolically, the date that began Fidel's revolution against the Government of Fulgencio Batista.

Hemingway correctly predicted that if the "veintiseis de Julio hombres". (26th of July Men) reached the sugar county of Santa Clara, Cuba moving from the east to the west, then there would be nothing to stop the Fidelistas from entering Havana. Accordingly, the Fidelistas marched triumphantly into Havana in January, 1959.

When the Author revisited Hemingway's La Finca Vigia, now a Cuban National Museum, he found that over 40 years after Hemingway's death, La Finca Vigia is still intact as it was the weekend the author was first there.

Sonja de Bowles at the gravesite on the grounds of at La Finca, at the first and most favorite of several dogs that Hemingway named 'Blackie/Black Dog". This initial Blackie was killed by Batista's  Federal Troops during a raid at La Finca Vigia when the Batista Government suspected Papa of storing arms.

Sonja de Bowles atop the stairs of the terrace, leading to the front door of La Finca, where the famous (e.g. Ingrid Bergman, Spencer Tracy, Max Perkins, Gary Cooper, etc.) would come to visit the legendary Papa – and like authors – all had to step around the piles of animal droppings.

Located now at La Finca, "Museo de Hemingway", the PILAR plowed the waters of "Corriente del Golfo", (the Golf Stream) for nearly a quarter of a century without a

break, from the Yucatan Peninsula to Bimini in the Bahamas, with Hemingway reigning as "Lord of Rod and Reel" and master of the PILAR and all who sailed with him.

The addition of the fly bridge was the only major modification Hemingway made to the PILAR after he took possession of the vessel allowing that it afforded him an elevated 360 degree view of the sea, a crucial element when spotting and hooking big bill fish, especially when they breach the sea.

Floridita

HABANA, CUBA